Leaning into the Liminal

Leaning into the Liminal

*A Guide for Counselors
and Companions*

Timothy L. Carson
Editor

The Liminality Press

The Liminality Press

510 W. Walnut St. #552
Columbia, MO 65205
USA

www.liminalitypress.com

ISBN: 979-8-9891640-0-4
ePub ISBN: 979-8-9891640-1-1

First published by The Liminality Press, 2024

Cover image art: John Dyess
Book Jacket Design: Carolyn Dyess

At which threshold am I now standing? What am I leaving? Where am I about to enter? What is preventing me from crossing my next threshold? What gift would enable me to do it?

A threshold is not a simple boundary; it is a frontier that divides two different territories. Suddenly you stand on completely strange ground and a new course of life must be embraced.

John O'Donohue
To Bless the Space Between Us

Table of Contents

Acknowledgements

This book was born at the intersection of two big ideas.

The first is that the concepts and insights of liminality have much to contribute to the practice of the healing arts and its multiple disciplines of psychotherapy, counseling, chaplaincy, spiritual direction, and coaching. In this sense, the liminality model is pan-theoretical; it has multiple applications for many approaches.

The second arose out of the mutual work of North American and Ukrainian teachers, trainers, and supervisors who are devoted to training and equipping mental health counselors in Ukraine. The scope of that work includes efforts to address war-related trauma.

Let me express appreciation for the team of people that has made this project possible:

The Liminality Press, The Association for Psychological Counseling & Trauma Therapy-Ukraine, and copy editor, Nancy Miller.

Contributors are, in order of appearance, Corie Schoeneberg, Nicole Conner, Lisa Withrow, Kate Weir, Tetyana Ustinova, David Hammer, Nigel Rooms, and Debra Jarvis.

It has been a great pleasure to coordinate and direct this grand assemblage of gifted people. For them I am grateful. And I am hopeful that those who read these words will be challenged, encouraged, and inspired.

Timothy Carson

Foreword

Corie Schoeneberg

Corie Schoeneberg, Ph.D., is core faculty of the Clinical Mental Health Counseling Program at Liberty University, Founding Director of the Play Therapy Training Institute at the University of Central Missouri, and Founding Director of the Clinical Psychology and Psychotherapy for Children and Adolescents Postgraduate Certificate Program at the Ukrainian Institute for Education in Psychology and Counseling.

I sat in front of my computer screen trying to stave off the rumblings of ensuing panic as I prepared for the most emotionally intense and challenging meeting of my professional career. As my Zoom screen populated with participant after participant, my sense of being overwhelmed increased with each face that appeared. It was March 2022, and Russia had just invaded Ukraine.

At that time, I was serving as the Founding Director of the Child and Adolescent Mental Health Counseling Program at the Ukrainian Institute for Education in Psychology and Counseling, which began in the fall of 2018. As an American specialist in child mental health, I was drawn to serving the Ukrainian professional community of psychologists with the mission to bolster psychology training and education standards. The goals were to improve the quality of mental health services provided for Ukrainian children and grow the number of competent psychologists prepared to address the already-existing crisis levels of trauma in the Ukrainian population.

On that night in March, I organized an emergency training on Zoom for our group of Ukrainian psychologists. I wanted to help them to work with children who were undoubtedly reeling from the unimaginable horror of war in their country. As we were meeting, Kyiv and other major cities were being bombarded by Russian forces. No professional training could have prepared me to navigate the up-close impacts of war and violence. This situation not only affected civilians in general, but also my dear friends and colleagues who sat before me on my screen.

Though my imposter syndrome had never been higher, an even greater sense of emotion and anxiety filled my awareness. Due to the missile strikes, the Ukrainian government issued a warning and advisory for civilians to keep all the lights off at night to avoid becoming visible targets. Abiding by this critical warning, my Ukrainian colleagues joined that Zoom meeting in complete darkness, many of them hiding under blankets to dim the light of their computer screens. As their eager but grim faces appeared one after another on my screen, my stomach turned to knots. I knew, instantly and without a doubt, that I had very little to offer in a moment like this. As I looked into the eyes of those who were hearing explosions outside their windows, I became keenly aware that my prepared PowerPoint seemed like an insensitive joke; my presentation was not what my colleagues needed. They needed something deeper and much, much more important. At the time, I didn't have words to name what I was sensing, but I knew I *had* to attend to it.

Compelled by an unidentifiable intuition, I ditched my plan and began the Zoom meeting far differently than I originally intended. Peering into the eerie computer screen light in the darkness, I was convinced that the place to begin was with connection and a sense of refuge for my colleagues. To do this, I guided them through the idea that instead of meeting under these horrific circumstances, we would imagine that we were gathering at the home of one of my Ukrainian colleagues' grandmothers. I shared the image of this grandmother's house situated in a lush, wooded area in the countryside of Ukraine. We imagined that the day was bright, the temperature perfect, and all the children were outside playing. From inside the house, we could hear the children's laughter as we gathered around grandmother's long kitchen table. With open windows, experiencing the fresh breeze and joyful sounds outside, we took our seats at the table, and smelled the delicious Ukrainian borscht that was placed before us in steaming bowls. We were all meant to be there.

As we closed this imagined scene, I explained that for this meeting we were going to sit together for a wonderful meal, enjoy each other's presence, and focus our table discussion on things that might be helpful. We all connected to this warm image and a profound feeling permeated our gathering. Rather than feeling terror under blankets, we now felt safe, connected, and at peace. Once we were inside the protection of "grandmother's house," my "training" transformed into an unforgettable time of community and learning.

I closed that first meeting with the image of us rising from the table and experiencing the sense of having our stomachs, minds, and hearts full and satisfied. We departed with the promise that we would be back together again for another "meal at grandmother's house" very soon. From that first night in March until the end of May

2022, we began and ended our twice-weekly emergency training Zoom meetings with this new tradition of transitional imagination. While I'm not sure how much my Ukrainian colleagues benefited from the information given during these trainings, I am certain that "gathering at grandmother's house in the woods" was the most important thing we did during those terrifying months at the start of the war.

As I mentioned earlier, on that night in 2022, I didn't have words to describe what my Ukrainian group desperately needed. In fact, it wasn't until I picked up this powerful book, *Leaning into the Liminal*, that I was finally able to name this important reality: *liminality*. The vivid descriptions and keen insights of liminality provided a whole new way for me to understand my work and experience. With the advantage of peering through the liminal lens, I could better name and comprehend this place of critical liminal transition, both as an entry and exit point, and how to facilitate passage for my Ukrainian colleagues during those very challenging days. I will never forget the power of it.

Significant moments in life need safe and sacred spaces to hold them. Something shifts inside us when we enter them, similar to when we cross the threshold into a holy space, a secret garden, or a hidden room full of treasures. For those of us who work in the business of significant moments like those that occur in counseling or chaplaincy, we must realize that we also work in the realm of sacred spaces, and it is the "ushering into" these spaces that we must facilitate before anything else. This is the heart of liminality. We must "cross the threshold" together with our clients, colleagues, and companions before any work can begin.

This powerful text highlights and emphasizes the essential aspects of making those liminal passages within our larger journey. My hope for every reader who dives into this meaningful work is that you will mindfully cross the threshold into those sacred spaces where you may discover connection and meaning-making. You are invited to gather around "grandmother's table," to learn and discover something profound for you and your work. I hope that you will mindfully pull up a chair.

Introduction

At the turn of the 20th century, anthropologist Arnold van Gennep identified broad patterns of renewal within indigenous, agrarian, pre-industrial communities. From his observations of the cultural rites and rituals that were utilized to foster those transitions, he came to understand a particular kind of social transition he named *The Rites of Passage*. That now well-known phrase became the title of a book by the same name that was published in 1909.[1] These rites not only fostered transition but protected the social group from the danger inherent in potential chaos during such transition. These rites accompanied almost every conceivable passage of life, including birth, matrimony, and death. Further, they honored the changing seasons of nature and marked disasters that afflicted individuals and communities.

The time and space when transitioning through a critical threshold is referred to as "liminality," based on the Latin root *limen*, which itself means threshold. In terms of rituals marking rites of passage, the movement includes a pre-liminal phase, the liminal middle, and reaggregation into a post-liminal reality. This pattern is demonstrated universally in different forms, practiced in many cultures.

By the mid-20th century, anthropologist Victor Turner built upon and expanded van Gennep's work. As he defined society in terms of a structure of positions, his model of rites of passage became one of structure, anti-structure, and re-structure.[2] A person or group moving through the rites of passage became a liminal being, a passage person, and was ritually defined by special names, symbols, practices, and dress. They were typically ushered through the process by tribal elders who act as liminal guides. The cohort of initiates formed a special community around their shared liminality, a status Turner coined *communitas*.

Because liminal persons were passing from one known and definable status through an entirely uncertain one, they could represent social danger to the community. Those who were temporarily outside the structure of tribe and community become ritually unclean, a social definition known today when people live outside social norms and expectations.[3]

Transformation through this passage was understood to have resulted in a changed identity of the initiates; they have passed through symbolic death and rebirth into new ways of being and new status.[4] The locale of the passage itself was a highly symbolized locale of sacred time and space.[5] Though the great transitions have taken place in chronological time, they are also grounded in an idealized timelessness, a time beyond time.

Though it is common for an individual or community to pass from one state of being to another, there are also instances in which the state of liminality becomes ongoing or unending. Some semi-permanent forms of liminality are voluntary; people choose to enter the margins of society and live in alternative communities. But other forms of permanent liminality are involuntary, such as one finds in the aftermath of genocides, life-long incarceration, or living in the social margins of society as an outcast.

As an individual makes a critical transition, what is experienced in exterior rites and rituals is matched by a parallel interior movement. The liminal person departs from one definition of the self and transitions to a new level of consciousness. The symbolic mythic passage is internalized. One becomes a new being.

In the contemporary world, these liminal realities take on many and varied forms. They arise through pre-established traditions or from a spontaneous response to events. They may or may not employ the guidance of identified liminal guides. The presence of community may or may not assist in the passage. And some forms of liminality may not include a sense of passage at all.

In addition to an unfolding liminal passage that includes beginning, middle, and end, other forms of liminality are not so linear. Some in-between persons exist in the margins, on the edges of society, a place one enters voluntarily or without volition. Other liminal states exist in the intersections, in the space where one reality collides with another, creating an undefined third space that can be the source of either great confusion or creative genius. In our present culture, liminality is often experienced at the edge of any predictable or recognizable social landscape: abandoned cities, empty buildings, ruins, VR alternative reality, and the dystopian futurescapes of fictional literature or film. The consulting room of the therapist can serve as a modern equivalent to a rite of passage. Movie theaters provide an artificially created liminal time and space, as do adventure pilgrimages of many shapes and sizes.

Our present historical moment includes vast social conflict
and dislocation, war and the aftermath of war, the rising
specter of an ecological crisis, the impacts of pandemic,
and an unknown technological future. Though people of
all eras have known liminal phenomena, the people of our
time have witnessed an exponential growth of liminality,
in large part the result of rapid and complex change. We
are living in a liminal moment of outsized proportion and
intensity. And the many forms of liminality overlap and
occur simultaneously.

An outline of the liminal process includes, in the broadest
sense, an arc of passage, a loop as it were, that includes
identifiable landmarks.[6] This arc is found in the great epic
stories and narratives of world literature. Its aspects are
recognizable in the content of dreams, the shape of mythic
tales, and the plot of film. And it is known, most of all and
most often, in the actual life experiences of people trying to
make sense of them.

The arc of liminality includes crossing dramatic thresholds,
leaving behind the old, descending into the darkness of the
unknown, wandering in the wilderness, living with
ambiguity and uncertainty, discovering new sign markers
for the future, and transforming by way of a metaphorical
rebirth. As a method, the arc of liminality may provide a
distinctive lens through which we may see and interpret
our reality. We also learn a new language with which we
can name our many voluntary and involuntary transitions.

The liminality model is process-oriented, describing the
ways in which transformation may take place. This model
includes an implicit future orientation, one which may
contribute a sense of hopefulness.

This book provides a liminality-informed model for working with those who are living in or passing through life-shattering and potentially life-transforming transitions.

It is to them that we dedicate our love and labors, for it is they who need this hope the most.

---

[1] Arnold van Gennep, *The Rites of Passage* (London: Routledge and Kegan Paul, 1960).

[2] Victor Turner, *The Ritual Process: Structure and Anti-Structure* (Chicago: University of Chicago Press, 1966).

[3] Mary Douglas, *Purity and Danger* (New York: Frederick A. Praeger, 1966).

[4] Emile Durkheim, *The Elementary Forms of the Religious Life* (New York: The Free Press, 1915).

[5] Mircea Eliade, *The Sacred and the Profane* (New York: Harcourt Brace Jovanovich, 1959), 191.

[6] Otto C. Scharmer, *The Essentials of Theory U: Core Principles and Applications* (Oakland, CA: Berrett-Koehler Publishers, Inc., 2008), 103-106.

The Work of the Liminal Guide

In traditional rites of passage, liminal leaders—priests, shamans, mentors, tribal elders—provide an indispensable function: they guide the initiated, interpret rites and rituals, and mediate traditions for a new generation. These ritual guides accompany liminal persons in such a way that they remain safe during transition, even as guides protect the larger tribe from the danger immanent in the instability of transitions. As those already initiated into the great passages, liminal guides serve many functions: elder-guide, representative of the ancestors, referee, and mediator of the spirits.

Though modern communities often have some equivalent to these traditional forms, including those found in religious traditions, many secular expressions of culture have created counterparts that serve corresponding roles. One of these modern counterparts may be the therapist, the spiritual director, the coach, the military leader, or the companion. These persons accompany those who experience separation, liminality, and reintegration phases of the rites of passage, and provide a secure container with ritual or patterned leadership.[1]

As those engaged in the healing arts, counselors, spiritual directors, coaches, and companions serve multiple functions within the role of liminal guide. They hold safe space, provide ritual guidance, and accompany their clients through a process of transformation. Their scope includes the healing of trauma, reconciliation in family systems, spiritual discernment, and the discovery of new hope and purpose. Those who serve in these liminal spaces excel most when they understand the nature of liminal time and space, crossing powerful thresholds, sojourning in the uncertainty of transition, and reaggregating as newly formed persons. Viewing and interpreting the work through a liminal lens brings added dimension to any school of psychotherapy or counseling, spiritual director, or coaching model. In this sense, the liminality model is trans-theoretical; its insights may be appropriated by any method of these companion practices.

Liminal time and space are disorienting. Compassionate liminal guides and mentors enter that space and walk alongside liminal persons. Guides bring the experience of having made their own dynamic life passages, so they notice, speak, and act as the initiated, ones who have done their own transformational work.

Much progress will be determined by the client's orientation to change. Those who function in a closed system in which external change is braced against rather than adapted to, find the most difficulty in the liminal domain. Those who live in open systems are more able to retain what is important and integrate new information into an ongoing and fluid process of change.[2]

Because different cultures contain widely differing narratives of transition and change, including widely divergent rituals and definitions of time, liminal guides must work within the framework of any given culture or context, including their myths, narratives, practices, social arrangements, role definitions, languages, histories, contradictions, and artistry. To be effective, liminal guides must know the culture of those making rites of passage from the inside out.

A liminal orientation provides an interpretive lens through which practitioner and client may understand broad patterns of transformation. The three stages of the rites of passage—separating from one state of being and crossing a threshold, passing through liminal ambiguity, and reaggregating with a redefined awareness of life—provide a framework for both assessment and shared work. The method provides an orienting map as well as helpful metaphors of passage.

The in-between liminal stage of transition is a time and space in which individuals and groups may engage in exploration, make powerful shifts, shed the skin of the old life, and embrace a rising identity and purpose. Wise counselors and guides help clients identify where they are in the liminal process, discover the movements of releasing and rebirthing, and embrace new thoughts, emotions, and behaviors. Liminal time and space provide the ritual container for the work of transformation.

A deep understanding of liminality equips the guide with distinct advantages. The first is seeing and interpreting through the liminal lens. The second is a particular method, a particular way of moving forward. The liminal guide serves at the *extremis* of life, where theory and practice join in a concrete way.

When liminal guides understand crossing thresholds and the nature of liminal space, their capacity to help liminal persons deepens. As opposed to simply returning liminal persons to previous states of equilibrium, they envision a

future-oriented process, a passage of transformation.
This liminal work is essentially communal; scope of
practice includes the gathered community, both during
passage and upon its conclusion. We who belong to highly
individualistic societies often miss what deep community
may provide when it comes to healing trauma. A rites of
passage model recognizes the need for community
engagement and connection. In the same way that pilgrims
travel together toward a historic pilgrimage site, and a
community welcomes them to their eventual destination,
so passages of the spirit benefit most by a robust
communal embrace. Especially in powerful experiences of
loss—natural disaster, mass violence, war, genocide, large-
scale chaos events—a communal response is essential for
return to post-traumatic growth.

A communal response may be made concrete in the ways
that counseling or companioning is concluded, often
including a sharing of learnings among those trusted to
receive them. The work of the liminal guide is most
effective in combination with the shared ritual of
communal life.

As the liminal guide enters the reality of the sufferer,
travels through ambiguity and confusion, avoids easy
answers, and seeks new wisdom, a safe space is provided
for transition, change, and transformation. When this
orientation is joined to a collective approach, healing is
amplified and realized on a deeper level.

Practitioners and clients often engage in an existential
search for meaning. When the quest takes one into the
depths of being, the great threat of non-being appears, the

specter of nothingness. Every shift from one state of being to another raises this existential threat, a staring into the abyss. Engaging in the courageous journey is often the subject of the narratives, stories, and myths of the great world traditions. It frequently includes a passage of death and rebirth.

> What we usually do not realize early on is that the invitation to let go is also and at the same time an invitation to a new way of being. There is new life on the other side of all initiatory great rites of passage, even if we cannot see or visualize it … As we cross the threshold, entering this liminal space, we die to an old world to make room for the rebirth of a new one. If we are unable to allow this death, we not only delay the process, but also invite additional suffering … If we begin to listen and allow for this ending to take place, if we submit to our necessary losses and begin our mourning process, we shall begin to move toward an encounter with a new life-giving reality. Before we get there, however, we must navigate the disorienting challenges of liminal space; and answering the call to cross the threshold into the transitional liminal container requires grace, courage, and no little curiosity.[3]

Regardless of the school of psychotherapy, counseling, spiritual direction, or coaching, liminal questions are relevant to every model:

How does one identify the thresholds that have been crossed? Are they defined by events which have transpired? Precipitated by a new developmental stage? Required as one shifts from an inherited worldview into a new one? Erupt on the scene without warning? Born of crisis? Slowly emerge as old structures wear out and die? **How does one describe the uncertain and ambiguous liminal domain?** How does one sojourn through the desolation of grief? What are some of the perils implicit in a wilderness journey? What must be left behind in the desert crossing? What hidden gifts and wisdom may be found in the liminal boundary lands? Where may unexpected liminal guides be found? How does traveling with a community of liminal pilgrims change the journey?

How is the conclusion of the liminal journey known and marked? How do we know that the journey has concluded? How is the exit of the process marked and known? What rituals are employed that speak to more than our heads, but also to our hearts? Who serves as the ritual leader at the end of the process? How are new discoveries recited and dramatized? How is the larger tribe involved in welcoming sojourners home?

Guides accompany anyone on a chaotic and potentially transformational journey with these questions, while providing a safe-enough container. Their roles are essential in the movement through liminal space.

---

[1] Jan and Murray Stein, "Psychotherapy, Initiation and the midlife Transition," in *Betwixt and Between*, ed. Louise Cams Mahdi (La Salle, IL: Open / Court Pub. Co., 1987), 289.
[2] Lisa Withrow, "Wayfinding to Freedom," in *The Liminal Loop: Astonishing Stories of Discovery and Hope*, edited by Timothy Carson (Cambridge, U.K: The Lutterworth Press, 2022), 18.
[3] Timothy Carson and Suzan Franck, "The Path of Initiation," in *The Liminal Loop*, 7-8.

Communities of Practice

What are the ways we can best navigate liminal space as both individuals and liminal guides for others? Regardless of the counseling, spiritual direction, or coaching orientation, several essential approaches are important, with the focus on "keep moving."

Settle in for the process. This is going to take time. Do what we can to emotionally regulate ourselves on the journey. Somatic-based practices help: Deep breathing, Yoga, Qigong, EMDR (eye movement desensitization and reprocessing), EFT (emotional freedom technique), music therapy, meditation, and prayer.

Remain aware of what is in front of us and within us. Notice without attempting to control or run away: mindfulness, meditation, prayer, reflective reading, guided imagination, ritual practices, journaling, and nature walks. Notice, name, release. Repeat.

Take note of parallels with universal narratives. Our lives are composed of stories, narratives written for us and narratives we write for ourselves. The process of liminal passage involves deconstructing and reconstructing those narratives. The great world myths and epic stories provide a wealth of universal wisdom for the journey.

Not only are these practices and therapies well-suited for use within the time of liminal chaos, but they are also exceptionally effective to use following the liminal phase, as one reaggregates to ongoing transformed life. The emotional aftereffects of liminal deconstruction may be released, and when a deeper mind-body harmony is attained, it may solidify new knowledge and clarity acquired during liminal sojourns.

When Michelle Trebilcock, author of "Hope in the Dark Passage," described her descent into the liminal cauldron, and the result of practicing mindfulness, meditation, yoga, prayer, and other spiritual practices, she put it this way:

> First came the ability to allow the questions
> without answers, then an increasing capacity
> to face pain without turning away. Next came
> an invitation to add curiosity and creativity,
> and, finally, a patience with living with what
> is, as it is, and letting the future unfold as it
> will.[1]

Case in Point: Narrative Therapy and the Stories of the Expert Liminal Traveler

Nicole Conner is the founder of Defining Stories. She is a narrative therapist and clinical supervisor who practices out of Fitzroy and Berwick in Melbourne, Australia.

Narrative Therapy positions clients as the experts of their stories. It is a respectful, non-blaming approach to counseling and community work.[2] Narrative practices rest on the notion that it is the stories we tell about ourselves that shape our lives; in narrative therapy the therapist seeks to collaborate with the client to negotiate (or renegotiate) the problem story that is experienced as negative. This process includes helping people separate their problem story from their identity by externalizing it: "The Person is not the Problem, the Problem is the Problem."[3] The deconstruction of a problem story also allows for the client to re-author the story in a way that "arouses curiosity about human possibility and in ways that invokes play of the imagination,"[4] leading to preferred or alternative stories. This therapeutic approach is also applied to the liminal stories, or, as I refer to in *Life Atlas Therapy*, "Liminal Oceans."[5]

Narrative Practices and the Liminal Oceans

Michael White along with David Epston first developed the narrative therapeutic theory, and often used the liminal rite of passage metaphor when consulting with persons who wanted to break from an addiction and/or from the excessive consumption of substances.[6] One of the

fundamentals of narrative theory is the idea that people
have many interacting narratives that constitute their sense
of self, and that the problem story they bring to therapy is
not limited to this sense of self but is influenced and
shaped by cultural and contextual discourses about
identity and power. It is an important part of therapeutic
practice to explore the "shores" of dominant discourse a
person wishes to leave behind in their migration of
identity. White refers to a predictable process when one
breaks away from the problem story, a kind of map that
emphasizes the phases of separation, liminality, and
reincorporation.[7]

In my practice we discuss the Liminal Ocean that lies
ahead, the preparation that is needed, and the "pull or
comfort" that a familiar, albeit problematic, shore holds.
These therapeutic conversations are often filled with
stories, skills, and knowledge learned in previous liminal
journeys. One person spoke of leaving the "Terror Island"
of childhood and navigating the "Treacherous Seas" of
trying to find meaning and identity in a different
"country." This kind of conversation allows for a
description of the stories that should be retained even as
persons break away from the problem stories that have
overwhelmed them. This rich telling and investigation
opens into the recognition that a person's life is not one
thin thread of difficulty, but rather a vivid tapestry of many
stories, including hopes and dreams.

The Role of Story and the Role of the Narrative Therapist

One of the convictions of Narrative Therapy is that personal meaning ("people make sense of their everyday lives through narratives"[8]) and action ("the stories people tell themselves are important in determining how they will act"[9]) are shaped by the stories we tell ourselves. Narrative Therapy often helps to make a distinction between the "involuntary crisis" stories of liminality and the "predictable passages of developmental and maturation" or those tied to "reoccurring seasons."[10] A crisis often thrusts a person from the known shores of pre-liminality to the uncharted Liminal Ocean.

Exploring the impact of the crisis that first delivered a person from the pre-liminal shore to the Liminal Ocean is an important part of externalizing the problem. It is an "unravelling process to reveal the history of the politics of the problem."[11] White likens the role of the narrative therapist in this process to an "investigative reporter" who is developing an exposé on the character of the problem. During this process persons begin to recognize their resolve and resistance to the problem and act on other values and hopes they hold for their lives.

The stories that describe Liminal Oceans are vital in preparing people for the forces they may encounter ahead. In such a moment, I often call upon the stories of others. These stories, used with permission, provide knowledge, comfort, and a sense of "not aloneness" for the person as realization dawns about how many others have also crossed the unknown Liminal Ocean. It provides a sense of *communitas*—a special community based on shared experiences, skills, and knowledge that have been acquired.[12]

An important part of the narrative therapist's role on the liminal journey is to engage "double listening." We listen for explicit stories and the "sub-stories" or "exceptions." David Pare says that double listening is "the practice of staying open to hopeful possibilities always on the other side of the struggle."[13] These "unique outcomes" or "sparkling moments" are the stories of events and actions that do not fit with the dominant problem story; they are part of the preferred stories. Double listening allows the therapist to ask questions that invite people to begin to richly describe some of the more overlooked but significant events of their lives that do not conform to the problem story. As clients are the expert of their own story, their voice and expertise are centered in these re-authoring conversations, whereas the therapist is de-centered but still influential. Through the story maps of consciousness and action, persons may uncover the meaning found in the overlooked and significant events of their life. They begin to "derive new conclusions about their lives, many of which will contradict existing deficit-focus conclusions" that have been limiting them.[14]

Conclusion

The various practices of narrative therapy allow persons who are navigating their particular rites of passage to re-author their lives in a way that engages their curiosity, imagination, and meaning-making resources. It provides liminal travelers with nourishing stories that include skills, knowledge, resistance, hopes, and dreams for the migration on which they have willingly or unwillingly embarked. The stories prepare them for the "'betwixt and between" that is characterized by significant periods of confusion and disorientation, and at times by despair and desperation."[15] These stories—told, retold, and richly described—become a compass with which they may navigate the unknown Liminal Ocean. As they reincorporate and land on another shore, they may experience something like that which another person described to me recently: "It has me feeling a new sense of home in this world that I didn't think could be possible."

One of the most extreme liminal states is that of a mass atrocity. The aftermath of mass atrocities is replete with vast personal and social trauma. When personal and cultural stories of terror are left unresolved, they often create an inescapable liminal wilderness.

Mass atrocities often result in disruptions that do not allow for transition. When combined with the later absence of truth-telling, transitional justice, reconciliation, or reparations, victims enter and remain in a revolving and endless liminal loop that has no exit, no escape. They are constantly reminded of the unimaginable in the very geography they traverse and inhabit. They are left with a

haunted past, unresolved present, and
unobtainable future.[16]
For the children of genocide, those who lost entire families
and were left as traumatized orphans, this is doubly true.

In the interest of providing a method of passage for these
children, Ncazelo Ncube and David Denborough of the
Dulwich Centre in Adelaide, Australia, developed the *Tree
of Life*. It is a narrative group counseling approach for
children who have experienced extreme trauma.[17] The
method is collective in nature; all participants share in the
process together in the presence of trusted adult liminal
guides. The tree—roots, trunk, branches, leaves, and
fruits—becomes a metaphor for resilience and growth. The
children are encouraged to explore their histories and
present reality, assess resources and communal support,
and identify future hopes. The metaphor is reality-based;
trees encounter storms and can be broken and harmed, and
it recognizes the way that a forest of trees can support and
protect all the trees.

Through art, storytelling, and shared reflection, a way of
passage is opened and the liminality that might have
remained permanent becomes transitional, so new
narratives can be formed.

Case in Point: Liminality, Trauma, and Gestalt

Rev. Lisa Withrow, Ph.D., (U.S.A.), is an affiliate faculty member of Bexley-Seabury Seminary Federation, a Gestalt leadership coach with an integrated neuroscience-based and positive intelligence approach, an author of numerous books, and a mediator and consultant in organizational conflict.

The interconnection of liminality, trauma, and Gestalt coaching can make a difference in addressing conflict, especially traumatic violence. Complex dynamics are at play in both individuals and among societies during times of great conflict and its aftermath; harnessing liminal space connected with Gestalt processes provides a path forward, unleashing opportunity to move from trauma to resilient meaning-making and reinvigorated identity.

Liminality

The in-between-ness of liminality provides new possibilities for transformation. Whether one is suffering from shock, trauma, harm, or choices that disrupt the current structures of life, crossing the threshold into liminal space by letting go of the past and embracing the emerging future allows for meaningful work of healing and formation of a new identity.

Bjørn Thomassen, a Danish social theorist, has explored liminality as a way to understand the movement through complexity of modern life. In his work, Thomassen emphasizes the importance of recognizing and embracing the liminal state without succumbing to the desire to rush past it.[18] In liminality, one stands on the threshold, the doorway, between the known past and the unknown

future. Experiencing liminality at that threshold provides a
unique opportunity for growth and reflection by
reevaluating human values and goals while still feeling
slightly off-balance. In other words, disruption requires
that one leaves some of the past behind, then spends time
"looking around" with new awareness of what is in flux.
As awareness rises, an emerging future becomes
increasingly obvious as it approaches from the horizon. To
move out of liminality with intention to be whole again is
to move toward that future and reintegrate one's life with
altered identity, deepened understanding, and a
transformed outlook.

Trauma is a very particular liminal space. Trauma itself,
loosely defined as an event or series of events that
completely disrupts the *status quo* in a detrimental or
deeply harmful way, can create a liminal space where
people may feel stuck between a previous reality that no
longer exists and a new one that has yet to emerge. The
experience of conflict and violence can be one of trauma,
severely disrupting familiar structures and norms. If
trauma is ongoing or constantly relived, that stuck-ness
can become its own new reality—forever traumatized. This
state of being can occur when war, sudden separation,
disaster, or witnessing or experiencing violence in any
form shuts down the ability to find wholeness, hope, or
employ human resilience. Perhaps this ongoing trauma or
disconnection (sometimes exhibited in post-traumatic
stress), is paradoxically the only "permanent" liminality
possible; in it, people never fully leave the past behind nor
arrive in the next space, but are permanently suspended
and uprooted or ungrounded. Addictions also function this

way. Living in such a state of ongoing disorientation becomes its own new norm.

For those who find a way forward, ideally with help and companioned accompaniment, the disorientation, uncertainty, and ambiguity often provide the environment in which they may recalibrate themselves, redefining meaning and purpose. Meaning and purpose are not always positive in their re-construction, but they do ground persons in a way that ongoing dwelling in traumatic stress cannot. For example, positive outcomes for societies in conflict might be a renewed commitment to values, collective action and cooperation, and a desire for peace. Post-trauma identity-building, rebuilding, or growth moves society through the threshold into new space and new collective identity. However, negative outcomes also are possible as people move forward: increased violence and instability are always possible as societies struggle to find new equilibrium and powers shift or vie for dominance. In the latter case, violence is likely to continue and becoming stuck in liminality is a high possibility.

Gestalt

For those searching for positive resources and pathways through liminal space that is characterized by traumatic experience, Gestalt coaching may be deeply helpful. In the 1950s, German-born Frederick Perls developed Gestalt therapy principles, emphasizing that people are capable of achieving wholeness and balance by

elevating self-awareness and personal responsibility.[19] To
do so, they must take an active role in personal growth and
development by working through various resistances or
obstacles that prevent reaching their full potential. One key
principle is the concept of living in the "here and now,"
mindful of current thoughts, feelings, and physical
sensations as they occur in the present moment. Indeed, for
someone living with trauma, focusing on the here and now
through deep breathing or repetitive, mindful motions,
rather than reliving the experience of trauma, can keep a
person from being overwhelmed during any given
moment of distress.

Conflict and violence are always occurring somewhere on
this planet, whether for individuals, families, social groups,
or nations. Those who work to respond to such trauma can
experience secondary trauma themselves. One result of
trauma for the victim and for the responder is the
fragmentation of the parts of the self. For example, most
emergency responders and active soldiers both see and
experience horrifying events and their aftermaths—and
over time, may get addicted to the adrenaline of entering
those spaces, shutting down their emotions, coping by
adopting dissociative behaviors like telling insider jokes.

In her book *Trauma and Recovery*, psychiatrist Judith
Herman describes the recovery process as following a
"…common pathway. The fundamental stages of recovery
from trauma [whether primary or secondary] are
establishing safety, reconstructing the trauma story, and
restoring the connection between survivors and their
community."[20] The trauma survivor moves from
disconnection and disempowerment to empowerment and

(re) connection. Integrating a trauma story into one's larger life story is highly liminal, and for first responders, it may create a new view of the world and their roles within it. However, participants must be able to take control of their own healing processes (with help) and make choices for themselves. No good coach will attempt to "fix" them. Rather, providing resources and adaptive coping mechanisms gives participants tools for moving forward through the liminal space of trauma.

In post-trauma environments, liminality becomes the fertile ground for examining collective narratives and shared experiences, and Gestalt coaching through deep listening and powerful questions invites these narratives and experiences to be expressed fully. Trauma-informed Gestalt coaching combines Gestalt theory and trauma-informed care, emphasizing safety, care, and empowerment through integrating or re-integrating mind, body, and spirit in healing. The Gestalt coach is a witness-bearer, standing in solidarity with the one whose human agency has been violated by trauma. In this way, the Gestalt coach validates the experience of the survivor, establishing a connection of trust that promotes empowerment. The significance of choice, in which the participant becomes aware of options, is one key element of this coaching. Through choice and personal agency, a participant decides whom she or he wants to be in the liminal and chaotic moment. This choice includes believing in one's ability to self-regulate and embrace the capacity for growth. Once choice becomes a grounding principle, resilience builds. The coach fosters an environment of safety, trust, and respect, co-created alongside the

participant's or group's definitions of what those
environmental characteristics mean in the moment.
Reestablishing, or perhaps establishing the relationship
between mind and body for the first time, introduces a
path forward where trauma is less and less in control of the
life narrative.

It is important to note that in the telling of a deeply
destructive or disruptive story, a person or a group may
relive trauma—and the coach accompanies them to keep
them grounded even while listening deeply to "what it was
like when. . . ". A Gestaltist helps each and all delve into
the meaning of experience, often conveyed somatically
first, then raising the meaning to conscious level. Once
contact is made (a Gestalt term for connecting with an
awareness), then people can move along a liminal path of
experience, heading toward the transformative change that
is always possible. Such a process of meaning-making and
movement along this path builds resilience and provides a
way to survive and eventually thrive. This movement often
includes accepting that pain is a part of life and allowing it
to evolve into deeper wisdom and ongoing resilience-
building.

In sum, liminality is the space in which human beings may
learn to adapt and embrace a transformation of meaning
and identity. Gestalt coaching accompanies and holds
space for the work that is done in liminal space. And when
this accompaniment is trauma-informed, it can deepen the
gifts of liminal space that are born of intentional inner
work, even when the disruption has *not* been intentional.
The growth of self-awareness, resilience, and holism
contribute to important reintegration in the foreground of
experience.

Liminal space and Gestalt process invite people suffering from trauma to reclaim their lives, discover inherent strengths in a choice-filled manner, and embark on a journey of reintegration, healing, and growth. Crossing through the chaotic threshold space with steady coaching companionship co-creates profound transformation, and indeed, new wisdom for the future.

Case in Point: Passing Through the Land of Child-Centered Play Therapy

Kate Weir is a Licensed Professional Counselor-Supervisor and a Registered Play Therapist-Supervisor. She is the founder of Kindred Collective in Columbia, Missouri, where she practices and teaches child-centered play therapy.

Welcome to the playroom. This is your special time to be you. You can do almost anything you want with almost everything that you see. If it's not okay with me, I will let you know.

These are the words with which I greet children when they enter the therapeutic playroom for a child-centered play therapy session.[21] They are not greeted with rules, lessons, or plans. They are not given instructions, ideas, or solutions. They are instead given an invitation to explore the room in ways that feel good to them. Upon hearing these words of greeting from the play therapist (the liminal guide), the child (the passage person), is ushered into the liminal space of the playroom. The child is immediately "leaving behind the old," the "outside world" in which children are told exactly what to do and how to do it by adults.

In the playroom, children lead the way. They decide what to play with, how to play with it, and whether to include the therapist. The child comes up with the plans, the ideas, the solutions, and the play. Being empowered to make all the decisions (within limits) is often foreign for children and can feel like they are both "descending into the depths" and "wandering in the wilderness." They have never been in a world where they are in charge.

Most children who visit the playroom live in adult-focused, adult-directed, adult-led worlds. They are told what to do, how to do it, and are celebrated and rewarded when they act, do, and perform the way that adults want them to. Thus, children often aren't sure of themselves, their abilities, and their preferences. It can be hard for children to be in touch with their essence, their true desires, or their honest emotions.

While in the playroom, children's feelings and ideas are welcomed. We do not do things for children that they can do for themselves. We don't ascribe praise or criticism to personality characteristics, efforts, successes, or failures. We simply accept them, neither condoning nor condemning, as they are in all their raw, unedited glory.

We, the play therapist liminal guides, serve as accepting, non-judgmental companions—ones who observe, with warmth and acceptance, what children are experiencing and learning about themselves. Feelings are embraced and not fixed. Resiliency is noticed, not directed. Boundaries are verbalized consistently and calmly by the therapist when they are needed.

Crossing the Threshold

The playroom is a place in-between: the liminal container. Outside the playroom lies the child's daily life—their interactions with peers, authority figures and family members. In the "real world," the child is often

defined by their symptom, their challenge, or their "problem." Outside the playroom, the child is one of many. Inside the playroom, the child is the only. The child is prized, delighted in, and afforded the deepest respect and non-judgmental presence by the therapist. Inside the playroom, the child slowly discovers or remembers who he or she is. Inside, children are apart from their tribe, outside the structure of their daily life.

Outside the playroom, children move back to their daily lives. But they don't return to daily living as precisely the same child who came into the session. On the other side of the play session, children are changed. Sometimes minutely. Sometimes colossally. Children have learned something. Unlearned something. Gained something. Or lost something that no longer serves them. They have grown a layer of self-respect, perhaps, and shed a layer of guilt or shame. They have been transformed through their metaphorical re-birth in the playroom.

Creating the Liminal Container

In the liminal domain of the playroom, the child is between worlds and between identities. This can sometimes be thrilling for the child, and they revel in the freedom. Often the child flourishes, almost immediately, with the invitation to be creative and free. Sometimes the child soaks up the therapist's undivided attention and presence and non-conditional acceptance like a sunflower turning its face to the sun.

Sometimes, though, the wilderness of this space is frightening for the child. They initially flounder without adult-led directions. They do not know what or how to play. They don't know how to choose. And it feels intimidating or anxiety-producing. It is strange to them that the adult won't solve or fix their problems. Sometimes it's terribly uncomfortable to be seen. In this instance the playroom initially can feel daunting.

Curating with a Liminal Guide

It is the grounded, accepting presence of the therapist that helps the child navigate these terrains. In the playroom, children are on a quest to find, claim, and take ownership over themselves, to remember their true essence, and to hear the whispers of their own, unique, divine calling. A quest like this can be daunting at best, and terrifying at worst, for humans of any age.

As children embark into a landscape in which *they* are responsible for their solutions and their decisions, where they are encouraged to look into the alligator eye of their emotions, they do not embark alone. They are accompanied by a wise, compassionate partner. Their liminal guide—their play therapist.

Their guide is one who will encourage when needed, but never push; one who will collaboratively assist, but never take over; one who always will protect them from harm to themselves, their therapist, or their sacred shared space of the playroom.

Their guide is one who will prize them and stay fully present, no matter how ugly and raw things become because ugly and raw is part of the beauty. Ugly and raw are the deep shadows in the pockets that we all have.

Their guide is one who *will* allow them to fail but will *not* allow danger to befall them; who will witness the tears, the fury, and the frustration *without* wishing that the child or the feelings were different; who won't wipe away the tears, but rather honor them deeply and witness all that they communicate.

Their guide is one who will witness, slowly over time, the most remarkable triumphs. Triumphs that, from the outside, might look like play. But on the interior, they are actually fears conquered and parts claimed. They are dragons slain and hope reclaimed. As the child gains mastery, the therapist will have a front row seat. Cheering. Celebrating. Applauding. But not praising. Rather, pointing out to the children what they have achieved, how they got here, and what they overcame to accomplish such victories.

Physics and logic make this truth obvious: To get to a new place, you need to leave. It's simple, really, and incredibly frightening for humans. Even if we really, really want to be in this other place because we know we'll feel better and we know we'll enjoy life more, almost always leaving the comfort of what we know is frightening.

Children who are perpetually frightened or angry or sad don't want to feel that way anymore. But to get to a place of more emotional peace and regulation, the child must take a trip, a journey. Every journey always begins with a process of leaving. Leaving what we know is much easier with a companion. In the playroom, children are embarking on a metaphorical journey, entering a "time outside of time." They are headed home . . . to themselves.

So how do we make the liminal, journeying part less scary? We create a container that is predictable. We maintain consistent and healthy boundaries that the children can count on. We bridge the child's guardians into the process by communicating with them and teaching them how to support their children on this growth journey outside of the playroom. We do this because the liminal journey is, ultimately, a communal one. And we honor the process with the greatest of care and respect.

One of the most difficult boundaries to honor as a child-centered play therapist is the boundary of anchoring the session to reality. We cannot encourage or support children's fantasies about the playroom or the play therapist or the process of therapy that are not real. This would be a betrayal of the great trust that children grow to have in their play therapist. Children need to understand that other children use the playroom. The play therapist works with other children. The play therapist cannot be their parent or their teacher. Play therapy won't last forever.

This boundary is so difficult to keep, especially for early play therapists because we don't want to hurt or disappoint the children whom we work with. Yet, the reality is that therapy does not last forever. Indeed, no relationship lasts forever. No process goes on without end. Grappling with those truths is hard and painful for kids while at the same time, it is necessary and empowering for them. They learn that they can co-exist with hard truths and painful realities. That they have the inner resources to cope with the hardest of the hard.

In the most painful moments, in the most frightening of times, it is ultimately our own inner resources from which we must draw our strength. Some of the scariest things in life are done alone. When we are digging deep, it is sometimes our own inner voice coaching us along. Helping children develop a connection to a deep well of inner resources is the greatest gift that we can impart through the play therapy process. In this liminal domain, this wide-open space in which children are fighting their alligators, slaying their dragons, and discovering their magic, they journey independently, but not alone at this stage.

Crossing Over to a New World

And how do we know when it's time to leave the playroom for good? Beautifully, it is almost always the child who decides. They no longer need this magical island, this oasis. They have tapped into the inner resources that they are using in their daily lives. They have opened their wings and they are in touch with their inner beauty, their resiliency, and their capacity. Their tribe has learned to empower them outside the playroom and to celebrate the beauty of this human creature. The child becomes an empowered individual in touch with his or her own capabilities.

Will they return? Don't we all need to return, at various times, to a home base? A sanctuary? A healing relationship? Certainly. Because the hope is that we never stop progressing, never stop journeying. Journeying will always include leaving the comfort of the known behind. During these times, we need a liminal guide.
Of course, the fear will be in taking the leap, a time and space out of normalcy: a sacred and uncertain time. It is during the leap that we adjust our wings and take flight to the next good place.

Whatever the theoretical orientation, communities of healing may adapt the core concepts of the liminal model to their work, interpret the process through a liminal lens, and then employ symbols, narratives, and rituals of passage that embody the inner movements of deep emotional life leading to resilience.

---

[1] Michelle Trebilcock, "Hope in the Dark Passage," in *Neither Here nor There: The Many Voices of Liminality*, edited by Timothy Carson (Cambridge, U.K: The Lutterworth Press, 2019), 67.
[2] Alice Morgan, *What Is Narrative Therapy? An Easy-To-Read Introduction* (Adelaide, South Australia: Dulwich Centre Publications, 2000).
[3] Michael White & David Epston, *Narrative Means to Therapeutic Ends* (New York: Norton, 1990).
[4] Michael White, *Maps of Narrative Practice* (New York: Norton Press, 2007).
[5] Nicole Conner, "Life Atlas Therapy Is Therapeutic Approach Developed for Story Exploration and Reauthoring." https://definingstories.com.au/narrative-therapy, 2017.
[6] Michael White, "Challenging the Culture of Consumption: Rites of Passage and Communities of Acknowledgement." First printed in "New Perspectives on 'Addiction'", special issue of *Dulwich Centre Newsletter*, 1997, nos 2 & 3, 38-47.
[7] Ibid.

[8] Duane Halbur & Kimberly Halbur, *Developing your Theoretical Orientation for Counseling and Psychotherapy*. 4th ed. (New York: Pearson, 2019) 2-4.

[9] Ibid.

[10] Timothy Carson, "A Liminality Primer." *The Liminality Project*. https://www.theliminalityproject.org/the-liminality-primer/, 2019.

[11] White, 1997.

[12] Victor Turner, "Liminality and Communitas," In *The Ritual Process: Structure and Anti-Structure* (Chicago: Aldine Publishing, 1969), Abridged.

[13] David Pare, *The Practice of Collaborative Counseling & Psychotherapy: Developing Skills in Culturally Mindful Helping* (Toronto: Sage Publications, 2013).

[14] White, 2007.

[15] White, 1997.

[16] J.D. Bowers, "Unending Liminality," in *The Liminal Loop*, 132-133.

[17] *The Tree of Life: An Approach to Working with Vulnerable Children, Young People and Adults.* https://dulwichcentre.com.au/the-tree-of-life/

[18] Bjørn Thomassen, *Liminality and the Modern: Living Through the In-Between* (Milton Park, England: Routledge, 2018).

[19] Fritz Perls, *Gestalt Therapy: Excitement and Growth in the Human Personality*. 7th Ed. (New York: Crown Publishing, 1976).

[20] Judith Herman, *Trauma and Recovery* (New York: Basic Books, 1992), 3.

[21] Child-centered play therapy is a counseling theory rooted in the work of Virginia Axline and Gary Landreth.

War, Trauma, and Healing

When war erupts in one's own land or at a distance and individuals enter the archetypal experience of being "at war," a profound state of social liminality emerges. For the warrior class within these societies, war represents a rite of passage. In traditional societies, warriors were carefully prepared and initiated into their roles as protectors of the tribe. As they moved from pre-war life to wartime chaos, they became liminal people with altered identities. Warriors assumed the danger and impurity inherent in bloodletting, a condition assumed on behalf of those they served. Symbolic ritual and ceremony accompanied all phases of going, fighting, and returning to society.

Warriors both past and present have emerged from those liminal places changed by that which they have survived, often carrying the invisible wounds of war. These wounds may include everything from the neurological trauma of explosions and deaths to the moral injury of witnessing or committing the violation of a moral code. Though this passage includes hardship and loss, it does not necessarily continue as an unresolved trauma. In traditional societies, when warriors received accompaniment by the tribe and its traditions, they benefited from an emotional shield that insulated them. The warriors were never left to transition by themselves.[1]

In the modern world, many of the ancient rituals and traditions of sending and returning are absent, leaving warriors, who are often transported from battle to hometown in a remarkably short period of time, unable to adjust.

> Without rituals of sending and return,
> elder leadership by the initiated, and time
> to adjust to a new state of being, warriors
> are much less likely to return to civilian
> life as whole persons. . .. Without those
> communal mechanisms of return, they
> become stuck in an involuntary state of
> permanent liminality, a war that never
> ends, and a war they can never leave.[2]

An essential aspect of the rites of passage model and liminal transitional space is communal ritual. Ritual involves the whole person in every dimension: mind, body, and spirit. Most of all, ritual is not something that one simply thinks about; it is based on action, drama, and performance. "You cannot read or speak ritual; you must do ritual; and that doing generates a surplus of meaning."[3]

Since it is not uncommon for warriors to experience an intense connection to the tribe with whom they have served, they may feel estranged and isolated when they return to civilian society. If war has become a new artificial world, departure from it may create its own kind of liminality.[4]

In our own time, we may learn from the rites of passage practiced by our ancestors. The way back for warriors includes a well-established sense of community, liminal leadership by elders, mechanisms for purification and healing of the soul, and opportunities for storytelling. These communal provisions forestall a protracted liminality of re-entry.

"In this way, the inevitable liminality of war may avoid becoming permanent, and what should be the solace of homecoming may not become a second liminality – sometimes deadlier than the first."[5]

Case in Point: War Affects Everyone

Tetyana Ustinova is a psychologist in Kyiv, Ukraine.

It has been said this statement is an actual curse: "May you live in an era of change!" For those who have lived in dramatic times of change, it is understandable. Starting over is very hard.

I was born in 1967 and for most of my conscious life I have lived during times of dramatic change. Learning and adapting is essential to survival, of course. This often requires an expansion of our consciousness and horizons.

I remember when Ukraine gained independence after the collapse of the Soviet Union in 1991. I remember how surprised people were that it happened so peacefully, especially since independence is often won with much blood and loss. Some hoped this would spell the end of such losses, considering that we had endured for almost 400 years, starting with the Russian Empire. How mistaken we were.

In my professional life I worked as a teacher, social worker, marketer, and coordinator of social projects. I approached all these professions from a humanistic set of values. That work continued until I ceased being an employee and began my own business. I was 45 years old, had accumulated certain achievements, and was interested in learning new things. I gained new experience and started to see difficulties in my life as new opportunities. I could never have imagined that in only a couple of years after striking out on this new adventure, securing some semblance of stability, and beginning to enjoy life, that a war would start.

In 2013, the Revolution of Dignity began in Ukraine. I was
not an active participant. At the time, it seemed to me that
the evolutionary path was better than the revolutionary
one. However, I went to the city center and began to help.
But then the first peaceful, young, and unarmed protesters
were killed. Until then, I had a business that cooperated
with various companies, particularly with Russian ones. I
was at the threshold of change again. If I made the decision
to end cooperation with invading forces, I stood to lose
much, but not nearly as much as mothers and wives who
lost relatives killed by Russian special forces during the
protest.

Just as I experienced the problematic consequences of
ceasing to do business with the enemy, the Russian
Federation began armed aggression in the east of my
country. Those actions precipitated a huge humanitarian
disaster. My world wasn't only changing, it was being
destroyed. Everything was reset. I had no idea how to
continue living. No one did. It was as though the traumatic
event pushed us off a high mountain and we fell into a
deep pit, broken and without understanding how to
proceed.

I hardly remember 2014. It was an abyss. I hardly left the
house. Looking back now, it may have been my son's
support that saved me. Among other things, he told me
that my strength had always been helping others. I took his
words to heart. So, in 2015, for the first time, I left the
security of my own home and entered a war zone with a
humanitarian mission.

I figured out how to help people who found themselves
without a roof over their heads, without water and food.
While helping the civilian residents, I got to know the

military, who also helped feed and rescue people and animals. With the money left over from my business, I bought and transported food, water, and medicine to the war zone, where people still lived, and transported animals in the opposite direction.

I remember my first trip like this: After arriving, I unloaded the groceries and returned quickly through dense shelling. Suddenly, I saw four large dogs trying to hide in a yard where a house had been destroyed. I already had two cats in my car, and I did not know how everyone would get along with each other. The dogs easily followed me. The cats sat quietly. For almost 10 hours on the way back, they lay in the car, did not ask to get out, did not pay attention to each other, refused food, and only drank water. I was a little worried what I would do with them all, but good people helped me and quickly sorted out the animals. In future trips I felt more confident and would counsel the animals on the way: *Are you scared, my friends? Don't worry, I am too!*

In the beginning of my work, I got to know everyone who was at ground zero, what the military called the zone of active hostilities. But every time I returned with the various requests for supplies and personal items, more soldiers had died. I finally stopped asking what their names were, who they were and where they were from. It was the only way I could protect my heart from the pain and keep doing the work. I just brought what was needed, unloaded, and quickly drove away.

War is fear, extreme temperatures, terrible smells, flies, rodents, abandoned animals, unburied human bodies, destroyed houses, an unending list of terrible things. But war has another side. It is also victory and courage, a heightened sense of justice, and people giving their lives for freedom. They lost friends, held on, and said they would mourn after the victory. Some of these have not left their military service since 2014, because they were afraid that their comrades might die because of their absence. Life did not stop. And the struggle continues.

A recent study of the impact of war on Ukrainian service women identifies the need for the correction and prevention of stress disorders and proposes a four-part model that includes solutions that are highly communal in nature.[6]

Combat stress affects and destabilizes the totality of the human being, a psycho/somatic/social complex of stressful states. The extreme conditions of combat often undermine typical functioning and coping, "depleting the adaptation reserves of the body," and "increases the risk of disintegration of mental functions and the development of maladaptive states."[7]

These challenges create barriers to combat readiness and performance, as well as contributing to difficulties in reintegrating women veterans into civilian life. The risk is often amplified by citizens' lack of understanding of female veterans. To address this challenge, those working with female veterans must engage in both prevention and correction.

The result of combat-related stress disorders is well-known: depression, anxiety, inability to relax, survivor's guilt, cognitive disorders, insomnia, and more. The recommended package of therapeutic approaches is also familiar: CBT, art therapy, Biofeedback, EMDR, and other trauma-informed therapies.

What is new in the results and recommendations of this study is an overarching schema, a therapeutic patter. This broad pattern includes four facets:

1.   Psychological/Physiological preparation.
2.   Monitoring and support during combat operations.
3.   Preparation for exiting the war zone.
4.   Psychological/Physiological readaptation after demobilization.

In other words, the soldier or participant is prepared by leaders/mentors for what is to come; monitored during the time of war; observed during war for signs of combat stress; prepared for exiting the war zone; and as veteran, helped to readjust to civilian life.

The model recognizes the need for proactive mentoring and support at each point of the process. This approach provides an alternative to an absence of support, especially before and after engagement in battle. It insists that the presence of communal/social support is essential at every turn. "The basis of medical and psychological support for women veterans is the creation of a re-adaption atmosphere focused on the public recognition of the social significance of participating in combat."[8]

The reentry phase must also be communal and include the "creation of a new cognitive model of living; psychosocial reintegration; adaptation to new living conditions; formation of additional sources of psychosocial support."[9]

In other words, a new mental map must be acquired, not only for the veteran, but by the community surrounding the veteran. Those returning from war need to be accompanied, welcomed, and supported as they adjust to the new phase of civilian life after war.

The four parts of this therapeutic pattern parallel the Rites of Passage, with pre-war preparation, crossing the threshold into war, war itself, reaggregation out of war, and adjustment to the new reality of post-war life. The entire passage needs to be accompanied by liminal guides and include a strong communal presence throughout.

Case in Point: Circles of Trust and Renewal for PTSD and Moral Injury

R. David Hammer, Ph.D., is Professor Emeritus at the University of Missouri and a U.S. Marine Corps Combat Veteran who works with veterans experiencing the invisible wounds of war.

Introduction

War and its consequences are part of the human experience. Every culture contains historic accounts of ancestors' battles with enemies, and many include myths of war among ancient gods and deities. Psychological impacts of war on civilians and combatants have always affected survivors. The first recorded accounts of the impacts of combat upon a warrior, and the long path to acceptance and managing them, are Homer's *The Iliad* and *The Odyssey*, respectively.

Emotional and psychological burdens of war only recently have received serious attention and study by medical and mental health professionals. Post traumatic stress disorder (PTSD) became a formally defined and recognized mental health category by the American Psychiatric Association in 1980 in response to persistent demands by Vietnam veterans for treatment of their combat experiences and their post-war difficulties transitioning to civilian life. Combat trauma previously was given terms such as "combat fatigue" or "shell shock," and was the "elephant in the room" for the affected and their families. A common statement made by family and friends of American combat veterans of WWII and Korea is, "My (father, grandfather, uncle, etc.) never talked about the war and he wasn't the same when he came home." When veterans returning from Vietnam were publicly, often viciously, derided and condemned by citizens who didn't serve, consequences were deadly and lasting. An estimated dozen or more veterans committed suicide after the war for every person who died in combat.

Categories of Post-Combat Psychological Wounds

Post-traumatic stress disorder (PTSD) is a mental health condition caused by experiencing or witnessing a terrifying event. Symptoms may include flashbacks, nightmares, and severe anxiety, as well as uncontrollable thoughts about the event. The PTSD symptoms generally are grouped into four types:

Intrusive memories
Avoidance
Negative changes in thinking and mood
Changes in physical and emotional reactions

Symptoms can vary over time or from person to person, and often become apparent when the afflicted individual is "triggered" by an event or negative comment.

Pioneering work on PTSD was done by Jonathan Shay, M.D., a clinical psychiatrist with the Veterans Administration who worked with Vietnam veterans in Massachusetts, using both individual and small group discussions and therapy to unravel veterans' personal experiences and reactions to combat. He concluded that combat-induced PTSD is a wound to the spirit rather than an illness or disorder. The term PTSD carries a powerful negative stigma among civilians and creates a barrier to veterans' effective recovery and transition to civilian life. One could argue convincingly, supported by veteran suicides, that American public attitudes about Vietnam and those who fought there contributed to the negative stigma and adversely affected hundreds of thousands of veterans and their families. The challenge to civilians to whom PTSD and Moral Injury (MI) are being explained should be, "War is the manifestation of political and diplomatic failure. Can you separate those who went from those who sent them?"

Shay realized that combat veterans were displaying adaptive behaviors needed to survive in a stressful environment, both in Vietnam combat and afterward. For example, emotional numbing that is useful in a disaster situation is maladaptive in a family setting, and loss of trust enhances survival in hostile environments but is isolating in a civilian setting. Shay wrote, "When trauma survivors hear that enough of the truth of their experience has been understood, remembered and retold with fidelity . . . then the circle of communalization is complete," and healing and recovery begin.

As Shay moved beyond the concept of trauma as a disorder and regarded it as a wound, he developed the idea that many combat veterans carried what came to be known as a "moral injury." Shay and coworkers defined moral injury as, "perpetrating, failing to prevent, bearing witness to, or learning about acts that transgress deeply held moral beliefs and expectations."[10] Moral injury carries a wide range of adaptations and symptoms, and each combination is unique to the wounded individual because each has a unique personal history and experiences. The uniqueness among veterans means each person's story is sacred between that individual and the Creator, in whatever form that deity is envisioned.

David Wood, a decades-long embedded U.S. war correspondent, brilliantly summarized moral injury and compared it with PTSD. The below Venn diagram is adapted from his summary in *The Huffington Post*.

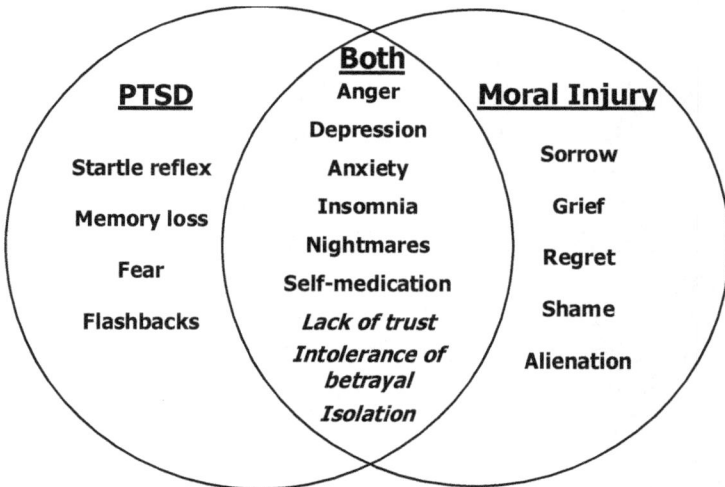

PTSD

Startle reflex

Memory loss

Fear

Flashbacks

Both

Anger

Depression

Anxiety

Insomnia

Nightmares

Self-medication

Lack of trust

Intolerance of betrayal

Isolation

Moral Injury

Sorrow

Grief

Regret

Shame

Alienation

Figure 1. Venn diagram comparing symptoms of moral injury and post-traumatic stress disorder. Diagram adapted from David Wood (https://projects.huffingtonpost.com/moral-injury). Symptoms in italics were added by Dr. Hammer.

Differences Between Ukrainian and U.S. Combat Experiences

Since World War II, soldiers from the United States have fought on foreign soil in Korea, Vietnam, Grenada, Kuwait, Bosnia, Iraq, and Afghanistan. These conflicts were not fully supported by the United States public or media, and only the Gulf War in Kuwait was fought with a clearly defined, quickly achieved end point. The enemy in these wars used civilians as shields and lures in combat, and U.S. combatants were frequently exposed to horrific scenes of carnage and slaughter of civilians in villages and towns. A common refrain among veterans of these wars is, "I didn't sign up for this."

When U.S. military returned home from these conflicts, it was to a society unaffected directly by the combat, ignorant of the carnage and consequences of combat, and distracted during the conflict by their own daily routines. Another common refrain among U.S. military veterans has been, "You were in the mall, buying a house, and starting a family when I was fighting." Only one percent of U.S. citizens serve in the military, and only ten percent of the U.S. military serve in combat. A veteran returning to civilian life from combat becomes 0.01% of a population unaware of veteran experiences. These veterans often feel alone and misunderstood, and coming home often doesn't cure their moral wounds.

Ukraine was invaded by a brutal foe who purposely and viciously has targeted civilians, including schools, hospitals, and subdivisions. All Ukrainians have direct, personal experiences in the war. Most have lost friends and family who have been subjected to the carnage of powerful explosives. Ukrainian soldiers will return to a population with a very different experience of war than U.S. civilians, one that shares both PTSD and MI as consequences. The dynamics of post-war integration back to civilian life will be much different and far more powerful and supportive for Ukrainian warriors than what returning U.S. combat veterans have experienced. This difference is important. U.S. military veterans who have returned to Vietnam decades after the war universally report that PTSD and MI are virtually absent there, where the Vietnamese fought on their land for their people and culture. Vietnamese civilians and combatants were in war together and they healed together. It's reasonable to expect a similar dynamic in the Ukraine.

The symptoms and healing modalities of MI and PTSD are the same everywhere. The first steps in recovery from wounds of the soul and spirit include eliminating self-blame for unspeakable events that could not be prevented, developing a supporting community, and finding a post-war occupation that is rewarding and further serves the home community.[11] Those who fight in their homeland, for their homeland, do not have to rebuild a personal community of support after war, and their friends and family have personal experiences of war's consequences and depravities.

Circles of Trust and Renewal as a First Step in War Trauma Recovery

The collective human experience has produced a rich literature and cultural heritage of overcoming and managing tragedy, personal loss, and depression. A common theme of this literature is that one must acknowledge the psychological wounds of war and depression, do the personal work of understanding why one reacts to triggers and encouragement, and "do the work" of therapy, understanding, and personal growth. The basic goal is "Don't stay stuck" and regard trauma as an opportunity for growth. "Accept this permanent but malleable change as an opportunity to learn and grow in ways not otherwise possible,"[12] and, "If we don't transform our pain, we surely will transmit it."[13]

Suicides among U.S. combat veterans of the wars in Iraq and Afghanistan caused Dr. Carson and Dr. Hammer to create *All the Way Home* in Missouri, USA, to raise public awareness about moral injury and to encourage veterans to "touch their MI wounds" by telling their combat stories. Research revealed an organization in Ohio (*Warriors Journey Home*--https://wjhm.org/) using ritual and trust to create a sacred setting within which veterans could tell their stories without judgment or unsolicited advice. We received training from them to understand the process and adapted the approach to create "Circles of Trust and Renewal" to stimulate veterans to get professional treatment at a Veterans' Affairs hospital. The ritual space of the circle provides the necessary containment of liminal space for healing. A liminal dilemma always requires a liminal solution, and that is what the circles provide.

The circles include Native American rituals based on spiritual preparation, cleansing, trust, and respect. A circle has no beginning or end, top of bottom, and is viewed as creating equality among all those who attend. Military rank plays no role in seniority, privilege, or conduct in a circle of trust and renewal.

The circle includes an altar, constructed to represent the seasons and cycles of life. Each season's color is on a ledge with a hole at the base of the altar. Yellow always faces east when the circle is created, and the circle is entered from the East to symbolize the birth of the healing process. Facing the altar from the east with yellow facing east, red representing the heat of youth is on the left (south), black symbolizes mature adulthood on the west, and white represents wisdom and elderhood on the north. Herbs are used in the ritual of preparation and trust which open and close each circle's discussion, and a "talking" stick, stored on the altar, must be held by the speaker. Participants can speak only when holding the stick. Sweetgrass, sage, cedar and tobacco, herbs commonly used by Native American cultures, are used in the circles. A combat veteran trained with circle rituals facilitates each circle. Before meeting the circle participants, the facilitator uses sweetgrass, a cleansing herb, to symbolically cleanse and purify the circle, including the chairs, altar, talking stick, and general area. The facilitator may pray silently in his/her religion as part of the cleansing preparation. The facilitator also burns a small mixture of cedar (healing) and tobacco (a gift of respect to Creator) in the circle and the smoke rises to the heavens. Prior to participants entering the circle, the facilitator, holding the talking stick, explains the circle rituals and procedures. All participants are equal in the circle, but combat veterans are the focus. Participants form a single file line with combat veterans first in descending order of age. Non-combat veterans, also in order of descending age, are next, and civilians, in any order, complete the line.

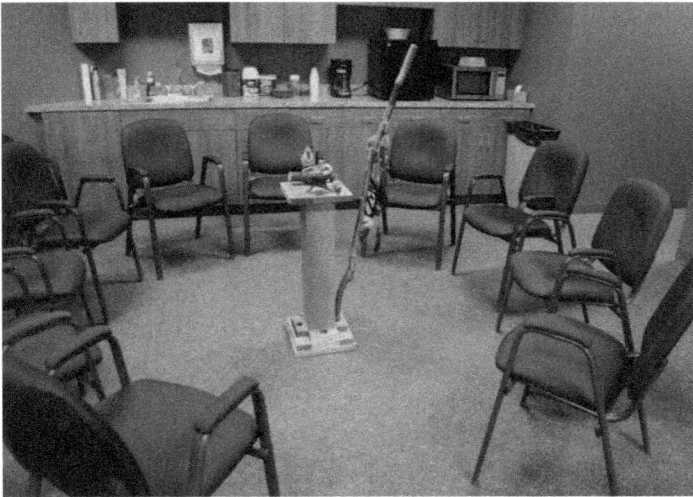

Figure 3. Chairs, the altar and talking stick used in Circles of Trust and Renewal. The circle opening faces east and the talking stick is in the north side of the altar.

The facilitator leads the participants into the circle. Participants move clockwise around the altar to select a chair. The facilitator stands before the first chair on the left of the circle opening as participants enter. Once all participants have selected a chair, the facilitator instructs them to be seated.

The facilitator reminds participants that this circle exists for hearing and honoring the veterans' sacred, experiential stories, without judgment or suggestions.

Religious philosophy is not in the ritual, but the facilitator explains that he or she will read an uplifting poem or phrase to set the tone of hope for healing and achieving personal peace after combat to create a tone of spirituality, honoring and addressing wounds to the spirit. After the opening statement, the facilitator provides a small dish of sage oil. After taking his/her seat, and still possessing the talking stick, the facilitator dips a finger into the sage oil and "smudges" his/her forehead, which symbolically cleanses the mind in preparation for focus on the stories.

The facilitator informs the participants that they may pray silently to the deity of their choice while smudging. After smudging, the facilitator looks individually into the eyes of each participant, proceeding from left to right. This individual eye contact serves as a sign that both facilitator and participant accept and respect the absolute confidentiality of the process. When the facilitator has made eye contact with the last participant, he/she announces his/her name and a simple background statement, and states that he/she is "clear" (of distractions and is focused on the circle). The talking stick and sage oil are passed to the next person on the left, and the entire smudging, eye contact and announcement of clearing is repeated until everyone in the circle is clear. The circle thus becomes a web of personal contracts and agreements.

The simple statement is the participant's first name and military affiliation. Civilian participants declare themselves to be a "person of strong heart," meaning their heart is strong enough and honest enough to hear the individual sacred stories, respect them and hold them in absolute confidence. For example:

"I am David, a Marine Corps combat veteran of Vietnam."

"I am Mike, a non-combat veteran of the U.S. Navy."

"I am Mary, a person of strong heart."

When everyone is clear, the facilitator returns the stick to the altar and announces the circle is open. In the event veterans hesitate to speak, the facilitator should be prepared to engage the group with informative information on moral injury and those who have used the circle to begin their recovery journey. This usually "breaks the ice."

When the facilitator determines that all the veterans who care so speak have done so, he/she announces that the circle is about to close. If no one wants to speak, the facilitator takes the talking stick and announces that the group will clear itself and adjourn. The group is reminded that the final clearing is the second contract among participants and is the agreement to honor the confidentiality of the circle and respect those who served. No smudging is used in the closure clearing. The facilitator then reads another poem or statement that emphasizes the warrior ethic of service above self. Examples of an opening and closing are included below.

The facilitator again makes eye contact with every participant, from left to right, announces, "I am David and I am clear," and passes the talking stick to the left and each individual repeats the ritual. When the last participant is clear, the facilitator announces the circle is closed, returns the stick to the altar, and the participants leave single file, clockwise around the altar, through the opening to the east. The facilitator ensures that no one is too emotionally disturbed to drive, and if someone is, the facilitator remains with that individual until he/she is ready to leave.

Veterans often are reluctant to attend a circle for the first time, but those who attend and speak benefit from the experience, and most of those who have spoken in *All the Way Home* circles have committed to counseling and other recovery modalities. Several veterans subsequently have informed the founders that the circles saved their lives and/or marriages.

Example of opening and closing statements

Opening statement recorded by a Catholic missionary from a Pueblo shaman circa 1848:

> Hold on to what is good,
> Even if it's a handful of earth.
>
> Hold on to what you believe,
> Even if it's a tree that stands by itself.
>
> Hold on to what you must do,
> Even if it's a long way from here.
>
> Hold on to my hand,
> Even if someday I'll be gone away from you.

Hold on to your life,
Even if it's easier to let go.

Closing statement – Tecumseh's prayer (Tecumseh was a Delaware chief and elder)

Live your life that the fear of death can never enter your heart.

Trouble no one about his religion.

Respect others in their views and demand that they respect yours.

Love your life, perfect your life, beautify all things in your life.

Seek to make your life long and of service to your people.

Prepare a noble death song for the day when you go over the great divide.

Always give a word or sign of salute when meeting or passing a friend, or even a stranger, if in a lonely place.

Show respect to all people but grovel to none.

When you rise in the morning, give thanks for the light, for your life, for your strength.

Give thanks for your food and for the joy of living.

If you see no reason to give thanks, the fault lies in yourself.

Touch not the poisonous firewater that
makes wise ones turn to fools and robs their
spirit of its vision.

When your time comes to die, be not like
those whose hearts are filled with fear of
death, so that when their time comes, they
weep and pray for a little more time to live
their lives over again in a different way.
Sing your death song, like a warrior going
home.

---

[1] Edward Tick, *War and the Soul: Healing our Nation's Veterans from Post-Traumatic Stress Disorder* (Wheaton, Illinois: Quest Books, 2005), 45-62.
[2] Timothy Carson, "The Liminal Domain of War" in *Liminal Reality and Transformational Power*, (Cambridge, U.K: The Lutterworth Press, 2016), 67.
[3] Mary Lane Potter, "The Body Leads the Way," in *The Liminal Loop*, 43.
[4] Sebastian Junger, *Tribe: On Homecoming and Belonging* (New York: Twelve Books, 2016).
[5] Kate Thomas, "The Two Liminalities of War," in *Neither Here nor There*, 83.
[6] Hanna M. Kozhyna, Vsevolod V. Stebliuk, Yuliia O. Asieieva, Kateryna S. Zelenska, Kate V. Pronoza-Stebliuk, "A Comprehensive Approach to Medical Psychological Support for Service Women in Modern Ukraine." *Journal of the Polish Medical Association.* Aluna Publishing House, Volume LXXVI, Issue 1, January 2023, 131-135.
[7] Ibid., 131.
[8] Ibid., 133.
[9] Ibid.
[10] Litz et al., 2009.
[11] Thomas, 2015.
[12] Taylor, 2015.
[13] Rohr, 2015.

Spiritual Direction

When a person passes through liminal time and space, ambiguity and uncertainty often provide a fertile opportunity for deep soul work.

> This attentiveness to inner essence or soul in the midst of in-between space and time helps us delve into the deepest of life's concerns: living with reality in both its positive and negative elements, determining our purpose for existing during our brief lifetime, establishing values that guide our actions and interactions, relating to experiences with other human beings and the natural world, knowing we are not alone and having human agency.[1]

For practitioners of the spiritual life, liminal spaces become holy ones, the arenas of divine disclosure.

> If the liminal is defined as the place between, the thin space where the normative boundaries of the small self dissolves somewhat, then the Holy can only be encountered through a liminal gate. The self-encountering the Holy is not a static entity …The story of the transformation of the self becomes a metaphor and archetype for the transformation of selves to come, of the tribe, and of the greater tribe of all beings…. In a liminal experience, just as we are between selves, so we are often between languages. The way we might have perceived,

> understood, or processed something has
> profoundly shifted ... human beings are
> perpetually in the space between the place
> they are escaping from and the place they are
> escaping to.[2]

In the Jewish and Christian traditions, interim times of
passage are frequently symbolized by the number forty.
Sacred time is marked by temporal beginning and ending
points. For example, the flood lasts forty days and nights
(Gen 7: 4-8: 6), the Israelites wander in the wilderness for
forty years (Exodus 16: 35; Num 14: 33; Deut 2: 7), Moses is
suspended on the holy mountain for forty days and nights
(Ex 24: 18; Deut 9: 9-11), Jesus' fasting in the wilderness
takes forty days (Matt 4: 2; Mk 1: 13; Lk 4: 2), and
resurrection appearances occur in a forty day interval
between resurrection and ascension (Acts 1: 3). All these
divine manifestations are understood to take place in the
seams of the story's fabric. The liminal passages we pass
through are identifiable and share familiar dynamics and
themes: the absence of familiar landmarks, loss of pre-
existing world, dominance of uncertainty, emergence of
threat, and disclosure of new truths.

Because the ways of the spirit defy human attempts to
regulate or control them, spiritual disclosure often arises in
unplanned ways. But spiritual deepening also occurs as the
result of long devotional practice, in which the deepest self
is cultivated over long periods of time.

> Some liminal spiritual experiences arise
> without any intention on behalf of the
> individual – they are spontaneous, even
> mystical events that defy all previous
> explanations of the ways of the world ....
> Other liminal spiritual experiences arise as a

> hoped-for consequence of an intentional
> spiritual practice.[3]

The stage upon which spiritual disclosure and
apprehension often occurs is a liminal one, the in-between
spaces that are not part of conscious control or expectation.

> Liminality is essentially and always a middle.
> It is the moment of in-between-ness where
> what has been is gone, but what will be has
> not yet arrived. In Christian spirituality it is
> the moment of Holy Saturday, when Christ
> has died, but is not yet risen. There is nothing
> to be done on Holy Saturday except to learn
> how to die with Christ, in the hope that one
> day—but not today—life will be restored by
> resurrection.[4]

In terms of spiritual growth, the way forward requires a
relinquishment, a letting go of the old life to cross a
threshold toward the new being.

> Unless we release our grip on the old world,
> accept the invitation, and give our consent to
> cross this threshold, we shall not move
> toward a new state of being. This pathway
> requires more than simply tinkering with the
> machinery, shoring up the foundations and
> adjusting. It comes as the result of entering a
> powerful process of transformation, and
> transformations emerge through the sacred
> process of initiation.[5]

A sense of movement is essential to the process of healing.
One of the practices shared in the Latin American *Roots in
the Ruins* retreat for the traumatized is the walking of the
labyrinth. One crosses thresholds, leaves what was, and
proceeds toward the unknown liminal mystery at the

center. The uncertainty of sacred space opens us to new revelations and gifts of the Spirit.[6]

The archetypal symbol of a healing passage is the pilgrimage. The notion of spiritual pilgrimage takes on great importance as one figuratively moves from one state of being to another.

> In pilgrimage, an extended and often difficult journey becomes a process of separating from the given, everyday world. Pilgrimage entails stepping away from daily routines and expectations and moving with special deliberateness toward a place where one might be changed. . .. Movement away from the given world and toward a distant goal can create a wide threshold of transition and transformation.[7]

For the spiritual director, sacred things are revealed and discovered in the in-between spaces of life. Only the uncertainty of liminal space can free us from what we think we know and who we think we are to discover the new being, the new way, the new reality. Liminal guides dare to walk in the margins with the liminal person on great spiritual pilgrimages.

The liminal guide is one who has already been initiated into the mystery of passage; he or she may be trusted as an initiated one – one who has made parallel passages, knows the rhythms of loss and suffering, and the wilderness as one who has traveled there before. The liminal domain is a space of awe, terror, of non-being on the way to being. An intentional pilgrimage of the spirit may provide a way to the new home. The liminal guide dares to travel those spaces.

Case in Point: Spiritual Direction as Practice of Liminal Movement

Rev Canon Nigel Rooms, Th.D., has been an Anglican Priest for over thirty years and a spiritual director and supervisor of spiritual directors for over ten years. He lives and works in England and has co-authored the book, Soul Friendship: A Practical Theology of Spiritual Direction *(2019, London: Canterbury Press Norwich).*

Let us begin with prayer, perhaps where everything begins for us human beings who believe in a creator of us and all things. Jesus gives this teaching on prayer,

"But whenever you pray, go into your room and shut the door and pray to your Father who is in secret; and your Father who sees in secret will reward you." (Matthew 6: 6, NRSV)

We learn at least two things here, that prayer is a liminal act and that it is properly hidden. The one who prays, Jesus suggests, must cross the threshold of the room, shut the door, and meet the hidden Father in this hidden space—a truly "betwixt and between" experience. Prayer occurs, necessarily between heaven and earth at this *limen* or edge between the world outside the door and the worship of God which is always present in the celestial realm. The shape of prayer, therefore, is the same as all authentic Christian discipleship following our Lord's journey from heaven to the cross and back again (Philippians 2: 5-11) and entails a letting go, a threshold which can only be allowed to be, and a re-integration of the one praying into the world; this shape is liminality or better "liminal movement" itself.

We know from many studies of liminality that, for the possibilities it holds to be beneficial, liminality must be *leant into*. Hence, no doubt the title of this book. It is very easy for the one entering liminal space to resist this leaning into, often through some form of denial (like simply avoiding our time of prayer as we all do sometimes). It is possible to get stuck at any stage along the liminal movement from letting go, to letting be, to letting come. It is possible to bypass the whole testing process altogether and miss the opportunity for growth it brings. As someone has said, "The only way up is down." The same is true of prayer, for which there are very many pitfalls along the journey to prayerful union with God. This space is where the spiritual director comes in, for people who pray can truly benefit from the wisdom and experience of another who also prays. God, it seems, works through this other in a way that an individual cannot do on his or her own; we cannot direct ourselves.

There are probably as many definitions and approaches to spiritual direction as there are directors themselves. Indeed, each Christian tradition whether Orthodox, Catholic or Protestant has its own methods. Having discussed several definitions in our book, *Soul Friendship*, we came up with this one: spiritual direction is two people attending to and naming the movement of God in the spiritual life of one of them, for the ultimate good of that individual and the world they inhabit.

God our creator has a made a trustworthy and orderly world, despite its brokenness at times, and it is therefore no surprise that the shape of prayer is matched by the shape of spiritual direction. The spiritual director creates a boundaried space, whether online through a computer or

other device, or in-person in a physical room. The room is
equivalent to the space in which both director and directee
pray. The director is directed in his or her own prayer
elsewhere and supervised by yet another experienced
director. All these connections create the safe space in
which the liminal movement of spiritual direction can take
place. Each time the director and directee meet, the
directee makes a kind of pilgrimage—leaving the ordinary
life and travelling, again virtually or physically, to be with
the director. Here, the door is closed; no interruptions take
place for the hour or so they are together. The spiritual
direction room is liminal space itself, a sacred space where
God is present, and where in fact God is allowed to be the
true director, present and active in both directee and
director and between them. The task of the director is to
make and hold this safe space, in fact to hold the directee
in and through whatever is happening in him or herself,
and from God as the time proceeds. Beginnings and
endings are key to this boundary setting and the director
must pay close attention to them.

As the two meet, the liminal must once again be *leant into.*
It is no use staying on the surface of the directee's life,
work, and ministry, thus reducing spiritual direction to
coaching or counseling. The task is, as in our definition, to
focus on the presence and activity of God both in the life of
the directee and in the *here and now* of the meeting. This
focus requires going progressively deeper and deeper into
the depths of the directee's experience in each meeting, but
also over time, as the two learn to trust one another and
God. Stillness and silence will be part of this liminal space
since attending and waiting for God are foundational to
spiritual direction, just as they are to prayer. The director's

skills here are to be able to notice what is happening in the
directee, especially resistances and denials, in order to
gently lead him or her to examine what is going on in the
depths of the soul.

Towards the end of a spiritual direction meeting there is
emergence from the depths and a re-connecting to life and
the world before the time ends. Here one can anticipate the
future, even the promises of God as they come toward us.
The directee, having connected with the God who is, is
now able to express how that connection may make a
difference to his or her conduct of prayer, living out of
vocation, and even everyday life. Sometimes naming these
future *intentions* is a helpful moment before director and
directee part company.

As often in liminal space, time in a spiritual direction
meeting is experienced as elastic—there is enough of it for
the work of the day to be done. Time may slow down,
especially in the silences, and the pair lose the sense of
time passing; it seems as if they simply have "all the time
in the world" to do the work that needs to be done. At
other moments time may speed up, as when an insight
occurs, and the future and its associated actions become
very clear. The directee simply knows what must be done.

Spiritual direction as liminal space is also necessarily
hidden, just as prayer is. This does not mean, however,
that it is something private. No, indeed, prayer is always a
public practice since we are praying to the God of the
whole world. A good example of its public nature is how
Daniel is persecuted for his practice of prayer in Babylon:
he prays alone facing Jerusalem, but that action is a public
threat to the Empire (Daniel 6). If, like prayer, spiritual
direction is also a public practice, then there must be

accountability and safeguarding built into it. We know from high profile abuse cases (such as that of Jean Vanier in the L'Arche community) that where this safety and accountability are not in place, serious problems can occur. And so, there is a fine balance to be found here between the confidentiality of the liminal space of direction and the supervision and accountability of the director holding that space.

There is much wisdom to be found then in treating both prayer and spiritual direction that accompanies it as a practice of *liminal movement*. The principles of liminal theory that have been researched and shared in many other human experiences illuminate what is happening in spiritual direction and enable its promise, opportunities, and challenges to be fully realized.

---

[1] Lisa R. Withrow, *Leadership in Unknown Waters: Liminality as Threshold to the Future* (Cambridge, U.K: The Lutterworth Press, 2020), 36.
[2] Joshua Boettiger, "Ye Shall Be Changed," in *Neither Here nor There*, 48-52.
[3] Trebilcock, 65.
[4] Ibid., 60.
[5] Timothy Carson and Suzan Franck, "The Path of Initiation," in *The Liminal Loop*, 6.
[6] Elena Huegel, "Where Heaven Caresses Earth," in *Neither Here nor There*, 22.
[7] Kristine Culp, "Pilgrims, Thresholds, and the Camino," in *Neither Here nor There*, 32.

The Final Passage

In a sense, every great liminal passage is a reflection and foreshadowing of the ultimate, final passage, that trek across the border between life and death; for those who have such an understanding, liminality is a passage from one form of existence to another. Each created being owes one death, and so the experience of dying is a universal one. Reflection on this passage fills the halls of art, the pages of literature, the annals of sacred writ, the film of popular culture, and the dreamlife of those who notice. War is defined by death, a phenomenon that gives armed conflict a sense of ultimacy. Some people are even addicted to living at the edge of death, the only thing that provides enough intensity to change an otherwise banal life into something worth living.

Death shapes our perception of time itself. Do we feel like we have all the time in the world, like young persons on holiday from school, musing what to do with an endless summer sprawling before them? For the person who has lived more years than anticipated, time is fleeting, always passing, an endless stampede toward the conclusion. At that point, time is experienced in days, hours, and minutes, as when the time of death comes, breath becomes shallow near the end.

Beyond chronological time, people often experience a sense of timelessness before the inevitability of death. Time stands still or is redefined altogether. In that time and space between ordinary, ongoing time and the liminal region that dismantles our structure, calendars, and clocks, time slows to a kind of eternal present in which all time is folded into one infinite moment. Death takes us to this boundary. And loving companions often accompany the dying right up to its mysterious edge.

Case in Point: Death as Final Liminal Passage

Rev. Debra Jarvis is a hospital/hospice chaplain, writer, screenwriter, and the podcast host/producer of The Final Say: Conversation with People Facing Death. *She works, plays, dreams, and prays in Seattle, Washington, USA.*

We regard death, the inevitable and universal human experience, as one of the quintessential liminal journeys—a transition from life to whatever we believe lies beyond.

Death in the context of war is not only physical, but also includes the death of our former lives and perhaps even our former selves—our emotional/spiritual selves. And like most liminal experiences we can be transformed by it. Death is physical, emotional, and spiritual.

Liminality is about ambiguity, transition, and transformation. Death (in all forms) embodies these elements. It marks the end of life as we know it and the beginning of something different and unknown. Like other liminal experiences, death compels us to confront our mortality and question the nature of our existence.

War Is Liminal

Through the lens of liminality, we can see that war too, is liminal, an in-between time. We describe history as pre-war and post-war. During pre-war we are afraid war will break out. During post-war we are afraid our lives will never be the same. Between those two fears is war itself—the violence, terror, uncertainty, and fear that we may die. Whether we are escaping from war, participating in war, or simply surviving it, we are affected by something that is not our choice. The only choice we have is how we respond.

When I was a hospice chaplain, one of my patients, a Vietnam vet, told me he was grateful to be dying of cardiac disease and was not killed in battle. "I didn't want to die at the hands of another human. The anger, the sorrow, the absolute stupidity of that would have been too much for me."

War is one of the most harrowing and destructive human endeavors. It brings with it death on a grand scale. But unlike death from natural disasters, accidents and disease, there is an intentionality to war, the choice to harm and destroy one another, that makes death even more confusing, unbelievable, and horrific.

War is a conspicuous form of dying and death, but certainly not the only one. Far more people die for other reasons than war. As we recognize death as a universal liminal experience, we can approach it with the hope of transformation, finding solace and meaning in the face of mortality.

Transitional

As we approach physical death, we are having a liminal experience: we are neither fully functional and alive, nor are we completely dead. In this transitional phase we may feel a mixture of emotions, from fear and sadness to curiosity and acceptance. It is within this in-between space that personal and spiritual transformations may occur.

What can we offer those approaching death—either their own physical death or the death of their former lives? A comforting presence, physically, emotionally, and spiritually. This offering is not in order of importance, nor is it linear. Human needs can bubble up all at once or one at a time.

Some people nearing physical death want to talk about their lives, their regrets, their sorrows, their joys. Other people will not. Either way, we meet people right where they are with a kind of vigilant presence. We focus all our attention on this person even if we have only a moment.

This kind of witness and presence takes a tremendous amount of emotional energy, especially when it becomes clear that we cannot alleviate the suffering right in front of us. If we can, we must do so, but often, we simply cannot. So we witness and comfort.

People facing death often grapple with the tension of letting go of the familiar while embracing the uncertain. It is helpful to encourage an attitude of curiosity. Death can be so much less frightening when we approach it with curiosity instead of dread. We can encourage questions: What is going to happen? What will it be like? Will there be ice cream?

I cannot stress enough the importance of allowing humor when dealing with the dying. If we can create an environment of compassion and levity, it will allow us both to go deeper in conversation. Why? It helps everyone feel safe. We both know that if we need to, we can always come up for air into a space of lightness. It's very child-like and natural to talk about trauma and death and then ask for a cookie. There is often a rhythm to these conversations that is healthy. There is nothing disrespectful about sharing a laugh with those who are approaching death. In fact, it can be a healing balm. As one woman said to me, "C'mon, it's not the end of the world—it's just the end of *my* world."

In the case of war, death is not merely an end; for those fighting, it represents a sacrificial threshold. Soldiers— some willingly and some not—cross into the liminal space where their lives become suspended in service to a cause greater than themselves. It is a transition from individual existence to a collective identity. In the liminality of war death lies in the paradoxical state of being both celebrated and mourned, remembered and forgotten. The absurdity of war death insists on humor for emotional survival.

Ritual

Rituals matter. Death and funeral practices across cultures help us navigate the liminal threshold. Gathering, grieving, remembering, honoring—these things provide structure and meaning. Funeral ceremonies, memorial services, and religious rituals can give us comfort, closure, and a sense of community during this liminal experience.

"It's the period at the end of a sentence," one woman told me. She had to postpone her husband's memorial because of COVID. "Even though he's been gone for months, I feel as if I can finally exhale. I can finally move forward. And it was such a comfort to hear friends and family speak his name. Yes, I felt grief, but I also felt loved."

Even something as simple as a good-bye—a touch, a nod, an embrace, a recognition of what was but will be no longer be—makes a difference. A refugee told me, "I stood in front of the rubble of my house and gave thanks for all that it was for me and my family. But I knew we had to leave so I also said good-bye."

Transformation

Facing death often prompts profound existential reflection. On our death beds we may realize we have spent little time nurturing our spiritual lives. It may be the first time we think about our spiritual beliefs, our relationships, what our lives have meant, (and want them to mean), how we view the world and what we value. It's never too late to contemplate these questions.

Liminality invites reassessment and contemplation. Doing this in the context of war can make us face two truths simultaneously: humans are capable of bottomless cruelty and infinite compassion. We may feel as if we are drowning in a sea of grief and uncertainty. There is only one thing to do: grow gills. Like fish, we must learn to breathe underwater so that we can go deep and explore and expect to find something of value. We often never discover things unless we expect there is something to find.

As we go through this transition to a new life, we have to ask ourselves which we choose: hate and bitterness or love and compassion? If we choose love and compassion, how do we *continue* to choose it day after day? Because it *will* be a daily choice until it becomes a part of who we are.

Reintegration

Of course, I cannot speak with any certainty about life after death, so I will address moving back into a new life after the death of our old one. We may have found new strengths we didn't know we had: resilience, courage, ingenuity, self-sufficiency, self-acceptance. We will have experiences and memories, both wonderful and terrible, that we will spend a lifetime processing.

Reintegration is rarely simple. It can feel like putting on a new coat in a different size with unfamiliar zippers and buttons. At first, we can hardly get our arms in the sleeves; they can feel too long or too short or too tight. And how do these new buttons work? Why isn't there a zipper? Where are the pockets? Does the collar stand up or lie flat? How can I possibly wear this? We may even have thoughts of, "I want my old coat back!" But not only are our old coats gone, they won't even fit us anymore.

Our Ambiguous Role as Counselors

As counselors, we cannot deny that we are affected by events around us. The people we meet, the stories we hear, can bring up old wounds in ourselves. So we must care for ourselves in the same way we care for others: with great love, intention, and compassion. We must witness our own pain, remain curious, and have a sense of lightness about our own journeys. When we feel as if we are drowning, we know that the thing to do is to grow gills. Then we can relax and explore, knowing that the transformational work we do with others can cause transformation within ourselves.

In the haunting film, *The Book Thief* (2013), the omniscient narrator is Death itself, and Death gives voice to the unvarnished truth:

> One small fact: You are going to die. Despite every effort, no one lives forever. Sorry to be such a spoiler. My advice is when the time comes, don't panic. It doesn't seem to help.

> It's always been the same. The excitement and rush to war. I met so many young men over the years who have thought they were running at their enemy, when the truth was, they were running to me.

> In my job, I'm always seeing humans at their best, and their worst. I see their ugliness, and their beauty. And I wonder how the same thing can be both.

> I have seen a great many things. I have attended all the world's worst disasters and

worked for the greatest of villains. And I've
seen the greatest wonders. But it's still like I
said it was--no one lives forever.

This voice of Death is, of course, the sobering truth. We
live in an impermanent loop, and our entrance, as far as
the world at large is concerned, often is as scarcely noticed
as our exit. We pass like a watch in the night and are as
fleeting as the flower of the field. There is tragedy. There is
beauty. But for those who ponder life under a canopy of
the infinite, there may also be wonder and mystery.

Conclusion

The Counselor as Liminal Being

The counselor who dares enter liminal space with those making critical transitions faces an outsized complexity; in addition to the deep processes already present in the inner lives of clients, external circumstances contribute additional dimensions and layers of uncertainty. The liminal guide who serves within the therapeutic or "accompanier" container of liminal transformation provides many simultaneous roles: companion, ritual leader, interpreter, guide, healer, and teacher. Though such a conglomeration of roles is impossible to fill all the time, the counselor, spiritual director, or coach usually lives and works out of more than one, depending on what is needed and where the client is in the process. Regardless of the focus of any one of those roles, they all involve directly or indirectly crossing thresholds, making transitions, and transforming toward a new future.

Mentors are often chosen by the initiated ones because they are trusted, effective, and wise. The most important source of the client-counselor/companion relationship within liminal space is often the most obvious: the best liminal guide for the liminal person is one who has already been initiated into liminal reality. Though the liminal guide has not passed through precisely the same form of liminality, the passage serves as a close enough parallel; the process, perils, and potential have been lived firsthand. A tribal elder is already initiated into the mystery of liminal passage. That is how they accompany liminal persons with awareness, empathy, and a sense of confidence. A ritual leader facilitates passage by relying on their own experiences of passage.

Whether accompanying those experiencing great loss, embracing developmental change, enduring the trauma of war, searching for interpersonal reconciliation, making deep internal shifts, or searching for the meaning that transcends where they are now, the liminal guide draws on a multitude of resources: the shared wisdom of their tradition, the particular tools provided through the behavioral sciences, and the learnings that can only be acquired by making such passages themselves. Like anthropologists doing their field work, they become participant observers, voluntarily sharing liminal space with those who have little choice but to be there.

As stated in "The Work of the Liminal Guide" earlier, the liminal guide becomes highly attentive to these critical passages at the edge, border, intersection, and threshold. It is there that the signs of transformation often become most apparent.

> A thorough understanding of liminality equips the guide—whether that guide is a counselor, therapist, religious leader, spiritual director, or chaplain—with two distinct advantages. The first is a new way of seeing the situation or person through the liminal lens. The second is a particular way of moving forward, a method or approach. It is at the *extremis* of life where theory and practice join in a most concrete way. Thus, we believe there is the possibility of creating such a person as the liminal guide or liminal leader. . .. Once pastors, chaplains, and

counselors understand the crossing of crisis thresholds and the nature of liminal space, their approach with liminal persons changes dramatically. That includes their self-understanding of roles and objectives. As opposed to simply returning liminal persons to previous states of equilibrium, good enough levels of functioning, they appeal to a more helpful method based on the rites of passage. . .. The three stages of the rites of passage—separation from original structure, liminality, and reaggregation into a new life—provide a framework for both assessment and shared work. This method provides an orienting map for the liminal guide as well as helpful metaphors of passage for the one making the passage. The time and place itself—separated ritual space for healing—is instrumental to the impact of the liminal passage.[1]

I once had a student who climbed Mt. Kilimanjaro. She climbed the mountain with her father and sister. After she had completed the pilgrimage, I asked her two questions: First, what did you leave behind on the mountain? And second, what did you discover that you took forward with you? It really doesn't matter how she answered. What matters is how we answer, how our clients and companions answer.

In one way or another, those two questions underlie this entire reflection on the liminal passages we make with those who have invited us to join them on this journey:

What do you need to leave behind on the liminal mountain of transition?

What have you discovered that you need to take forward to transform the future?

---

[1] Timothy Carson, "Pastoral Theology and the Whirlwind," in *Crossing Thresholds: A Practical Theology of Liminality* (Cambridge, U.K: The Lutterworth Press, 2021), 201-205.

Bibliography

Boettiger, Joshua. "Ye Shall Be Changed." In *Neither Here nor There: The Many Voices of Liminality*, ed. Timothy Carson. Cambridge, U.K: The Lutterworth Press, 2019.

Bowers, J.D. "Unending Liminality," in *The Liminal Loop: Astonishing Stories of Discovery and Hope*, ed. Timothy Carson. Cambridge, U.K: The Lutterworth Press, 2022.

Carson, Timothy. "A Liminality Primer." *The Liminality Project*. https: //www.theliminalityproject.org/the-liminality-primer/, 2019.

Carson, Timothy, and Suzan Franck. "The Path of Initiation." In *The Liminal Loop: Astonishing Stories of Discovery and Hope*, ed. Timothy Carson. Cambridge, U.K: The Lutterworth Press, 2022.

Carson, Timothy, "Pastoral Theology and the Whirlwind." In *Crossing Thresholds: A Practical Theology of Liminality*, Timothy Carson, Rosy Fairhurst, Nigel Rooms, Lisa Withrow. Cambridge, U.K: The Lutterworth Press, 2021.

Carson, Timothy. "The Liminal Domain of War." In *Liminal Reality and Transformational Power*. Cambridge, U.K: The Lutterworth Press, 2016.

Conner, Nicole. "Life Atlas Therapy Is Therapeutic Approach Developed for Story Exploration and Reauthoring." https://definingstories.com.au/narrative-therapy, 2017.

Coombes, Elizabeth. "Liminal Pathways to Healing: Music Therapy with Young People on the Autistic Spectrum." In

The Liminal Loop: Astonishing Stories of Discovery and Hope, ed. Timothy Carson. Cambridge, U.K: The Lutterworth Press, 2022.

Culp, Kristine. "Pilgrims, Thresholds, and the Camino." in *Neither Here nor There: The Many Voices of Liminality,* ed. Timothy Carson. Cambridge, U.K: The Lutterworth Press, 2019.

Douglas, Mary. *Purity and Danger.* New York: Frederick A. Praeger, 1966.

Durkheim, Emile. *The Elementary Forms of the Religious Life.* New York: The Free Press, 1915.

Eliade, Mircea. *The Sacred and the Profane.* New York: Harcourt Brace Jovanovich, 1959.

Frankl, Viktor E. *Man's Search for Meaning.* Boston: Beacon Press, 2006.

Halbur, Duane, & Kimberly Halbur. *Developing your Theoretical Orientation for Counseling and Psychotherapy.* 4th ed. New York: Pearson, 2019.

Herman, Judith. *Trauma and Recovery.* New York: Basic Books, 1992.

Huegel, Elena. "Where Heaven Caresses Earth." In *Neither Here nor There: The Many Voices of Liminality,* ed. Timothy Carson. Cambridge, U.K: The Lutterworth Press, 2019.

Junger, Sebastian. *Tribe: On Homecoming and Belonging*. New York: Twelve Books, Hachette Book Group, 2016.

Junger, Sebastian. *War*. New York: Twelve Books, Hatchett Book Group, 2010.

Kozhyna, Hanna M., Vsevolod V. Stebliuk, Yuliia O. Asieieva, Kateryna S. Zelenska, Kate V. Pronoza-Stebliuk. "A Comprehensive Approach to Medical Psychological Support for Service Women in Modern Ukraine." *Journal of the Polish Medical Association*, Aluna Publishing House, Volume LXXVI, Issue 1, January 2023, 131-135.

Litz, Brett T., Leslie Lebowitz, Matt J. Gray, and William P. Nash. *Adaptive Disclosure: A New Treatment for Military Trauma, Loss, and Moral Injury*. New York: The Guilford Press, 2016.

MacEowen, Frank. *The Mist-Filled Path: Celtic Wisdom for Exiles, Wanderers, and Seekers*. Novato, CA.: New World Library, 2002.

Morgan, Alice. *What Is Narrative Therapy? An Easy-To-Read Introduction*. Adelaide, South Australia: Dulwich Centre Publications, 2000.

Nouwen, Henri. *The Inner Voice of Love: A Journey Through Anguish to Freedom*. New York: Doubleday, Image Books, 1998.

Pare, David. *The Practice of Collaborative Counseling & Psychotherapy: Developing Skills in Culturally Mindful Helping*. Toronto: Sage Publications, 2013.

Perls, Fritz. *Gestalt Therapy: Excitement and Growth in the Human Personality.* 7th Ed. New York: Crown Publishing, 1976.

Potter, Mary Lane. "The Body Leads the Way." In *The Liminal Loop: Astonishing Stories of Discovery and Hope,* ed. Timothy Carson. Cambridge, U.K: The Lutterworth Press, 2022.

Rohr, Richard. *What the Mystics Know: Seven Pathways to Your Deeper Self.* New York: Crossroads Publishing Co., 2015.

Scharmer, Otto C. *The Essentials of Theory U: Core Principles and Applications.* Oakland, CA: Berrett-Koehler Publishers, Inc., 2008.

Shay, J. *Achilles in Vietnam: Combat Trauma and the Undoing of Character.* New York: Simon and Schuster, Touchstone, 1994.

Stein, Jan, and Murray Stein. "Psychotherapy, Initiation and the Midlife Transition." In *Betwixt and Between,* ed. Louise Cams Mahdi. La Salle, IL: Open /Court Pub. Co., 1987.

Taylor, Sarah. *Just Roll with It: 7 Battle-Tested Truths for Building a Resilient Life.* Collierville, TN.: Innovo Publishing Co., 2015.

Thomas, Kate. *Brave, Strong and True: The Modern Warrior's Battle for Balance.* Collierville, TN.: Innovo Publishing Co., 2015.

Thomas, Kate. "The Two Liminalities of War." In *Neither Here nor There: The Many Voices of Liminality*, ed. Timothy Carson. Cambridge, U.K: The Lutterworth Press, 2019.

Thomassen, Bjørn. *Liminality and the Modern: Living Through the In-Between.* Milton Park, England: Routledge, 2018.

Tick, Edward. *War and the Soul: Healing our Nation's Veterans from Post-Traumatic Stress Disorder.* Wheaton, Illinois: Quest Books, 2005.

Trebilcock, Michelle. "Hope in the Dark Passage." In *Neither Here nor There: The Many Voices of Liminality*, ed. Timothy Carson. Cambridge, U.K: The Lutterworth Press, 2019.

The Tree of Life: An Approach to Working with Vulnerable Children, Young People and Adults. https://dulwichcentre.com.au/the-tree-of-life/.

Turner, Victor. "Liminality and Communitas." In *The Ritual Process: Structure and Anti-Structure.* Chicago: Aldine Publishing, 1969. Abridged.

Turner, Victor. *The Ritual Process: Structure and Anti-Structure.* Chicago: University of Chicago Press, 1966.

van der Kolk, Bessel. *The Body Keeps the Score: Brain, Mind and Body in the Healing of Trauma.* New York: Random House, Penguin Publishing Group, 2018.

van Gennep, Arnold. *The Rites of Passage.* London: Routledge and Kegan Paul, 1960.

White, Michael. "Challenging the Culture of Consumption: Rites of Passage and Communities of Acknowledgement." First printed in "New Perspectives on 'Addiction'", special issue of *Dulwich Centre Newsletter*, 1997, nos. 2 & 3, 38-47.

White, Michael. *Maps of Narrative Practice.* New York: Norton Press, 2007.

White, Michael, & David Epston. *Narrative Means to Therapeutic Ends.* New York: Norton, 1990.

Withrow, Lisa R. *Leadership in Unknown Waters: Liminality as Threshold to the Future.* Cambridge, U.K: The Lutterworth Press, 2020.

Withrow, Lisa R. "Wayfinding to Freedom." In *The Liminal Loop: Astonishing Stories of Discovery and Hope,* ed. Timothy Carson. Cambridge, U.K: The Lutterworth Press, 2022.

Wood, David. "Moral Injury," Part 3. *The Huffington Post.* https://projects.huffingtonpost.com/moral-injury, 2014.

About the Editor

Timothy Carson is a pastor, teacher, author, and editor. After many years serving as a parish pastor, he teaches Liminal Studies in the Honors College of the University of Missouri, USA; curates the Liminality Project (TheLiminalityProject.org); co-directs the Guild for Engaged Liminality (engagedliminality.org); and serves as the co-owner and an editor of The Liminality Press (liminalitypress.com). He is a TEDx speaker who applies the insights of liminality to popular culture.

Other Books on Liminality by Timothy Carson

Liminal Reality and Transformational Power:
Transition, Renewal and Hope (2016)

"Equipped with liminality, this book takes the reader on a voyage into the heart of theology, and into the human search for meaning. It is worth a read for scholars and non-scholars alike."

Bjørn Thomassen, Roskilde University, Denmark

Neither Here nor There:
The Many Voices of Liminality (2019)

"Carson's edited work intriguingly weaves together the academic and the personal in this rich and diverse tapestry of all things liminal."

Elizabeth Parker, University of West London, England

Crossing Thresholds:
A Practical Theology of Liminality, co-author (2021)

"Holding a pluralistic vision about the significance of liminality, readers are invited into an ever-expanding sense of a God at work in the world."

Joretta L. Marshall, Brite Divinity School, USA

The Liminal Loop:
Astonishing Stories of Discovery and Hope (2022)

"*The Liminal Loop* is an anthology rich in contemplative reflection on the human condition and the bends in our personal and collective paths."

Barry Stephenson, Memorial University, Newfoundland, Canada

www.ingramcontent.com/pod-product-compliance
Lightning Source LLC
Chambersburg PA
CBHW032101020426
42335CB00011B/435